Form is

E M P T I N E S S

is Form

The Heart Sutra

DEDICATED
TO ALL PAST, PRESENT, AND FUTURE BUDDHAS.
MAY ALL OF US, SOMEDAY, FIND OURSELVES
IN THEIR ILLUSTRIOUS COMPANY.

Form is EMPTINESS is Form

The Heart Sutra

Robert Wydler Haduch

Center for Zen-Buddhism
Zürich, Switzerland
www.zzbzurich.ch

© Zentrum für Zen-Buddhismus - Zürich, Switzerland - 2016
All Rights to author's original material reserved.

Cover Image: "Form is Emptiness" - *RWH*
Dedication page image: Avalokiteshvara - *RWH*
Image: The Ascetic Buddha: - *RWH*

All Rights Reserved.

ISBN 978-3-9524409-2-6

                                    I
                                  stand
                               at the peak
                              of the pyramid
                            supported by all of
                           you, named & unnamed,
                         that have passed previously.
                       To each of you, I bow humbly in
                      thanksgiving, offering an inadequate
                    thank you for the Herculean effort you
                  have expended steadying my erratic compass
                and keeping this barque afloat on the tempestuous
             ocean of existence. To all of the countless of you, I say:
             Gate! …Gate! …Paragate! …Parasamgate! …Bodhi Svaha!

I also wish to thank the three people who have generously contributed their time and talents to the "creation of this form from Emptiness."

First, I thank my wife and partner, Agetsu. We began our journey together many years ago when we married under the Bodhi Tree in Bodh Gaya. In the ensuing years Agetsu, as an acknowledged Rinzai Zen teacher, and I have co-partnered the Center for Zen-Buddhism in Zürich. Her critical analysis, based on years of study and "real-life" experience were of invaluable assistance in the preparation of this book.

Secondly, a heartfelt "*thank you*" to my dear friends Loretta Gesmond and Walter Reece for the time and effort they spent correcting my faulty grammar and for their many helpful suggestions and incisive questions.

…Gate! Gate! Paragate! Parasamgate! Bodhi Svaha!

Table of Contents

Preface	9
1. Bodhisattva Avalokiteshvara	13
2. Shariputra	17
3. The Telling	21
4. Words as Surrogates	25
5. Prajñāpāramitā	28
6. Can we realize Prajñāpāramitā?	30
7. Open the Puzzle Box	33
8. Good News	39
9. The soon-to-be-Buddha	42
10. Six Years	45
11. The Bodhi Tree	48
12. Under the Bodhi Tree	50
13. Doctrine of Dependent Arising	55
14. The First Noble Truth	68
14.1 Ordinary Suffering	70
14.2 Change	71
14.3 Conditioned States	73
15. The Second Noble Truth	76
16. The Third Noble Truth	82
17. The Fourth Noble Truth	86
18. Putting It All Together	91
19. What's Next	103
20. Heart Sutra	105
21. Maka Hannya Haramita Shingyo	107
Glossary	108

Preface

Monday, September 3, 1990, 6:30 am, upstate New York, Zen Mountain Monastery, the resident ZMM Sangha had assembled for the first meditation period of the day in the large meditation hall (Zendo). The Zendo was, at one time, a Roman Catholic chapel. All that remained of its earlier history was a large wooden crucifix that hung on the stone wall behind the altar. The man on the cross looked down on the assembly of black-robed Zen monks and students, sitting cross-legged on black, cotton-fabric, kapok-filled cushions. The Zafus (cushions) sat on black, cotton-fabric, one-meter square mats neatly aligned along the two long walls of the hall. There were fifteen "zennies" in each row; facing each other across the expanse of polished wood floor that separated them. Directly under the figure of the crucified teacher was an altar with a statue of another teacher, the Buddha. He was standing, a slight smile on his face, looking out over the assembly; his right hand held upright, the palm facing outwards. On the altar were vases of fresh flowers, a small porcelain bowl of fresh water, a small bronze pot with an already lit stick of incense and a candle. The incense smoke drifted lazily upwards releasing an exotic aroma that bathed the teachers and students alike. It was only moments ago that the monastery's abbot had lit the incense stick from the dancing candle flame and with a deep bow had placed it into the bronze pot.

Our teacher stood in front of the carved images of the two teachers and looked out at the silent assembly. From a discretely located assortment of gongs, mokugyos (wooden percussion instruments in the shape of a fish-head) and other assorted musical instruments, unique to a Zen monastery, had come the "wake-up" sound of an inkin (a brass bell); struck by one of the senior monks. Three times he had struck the inkin. The brilliant sound had immediately driven away any feelings of sleepiness from one's brain. At the sound of the inkin, we had all stood in unison. With our sutra-chanting books in hand, we waited to begin the recitation of the first chant.

The teacher began with the words: **"Maha Prajñāpāramitā Heart Sūtra."** Our collective voice had joined his with:

> *"The Bodhisattva Avalokiteshvara*
> *actively engaged in Prajñāpāramitā,*
> *clearly saw the Five Skandhas to be empty, thus*
> *completely overcoming Ignorance.*
>
> *O Shariputra, form is no other than Emptiness.*
> *Emptiness is no other than form. Form is exactly*
> *Emptiness. Emptiness is exactly form. The same is true*
> *for sensation, perception, volitional formations,*
> *consciousness. ..."*

It was the first time in my life that I had heard the *Heart Sutra* chanted. Indeed, it was the first time in my life I even knew something called the *Heart Sutra* existed. Hearing the words chanted; reading them for myself out of the sutra book was, literally, a mind-blowing experience. It was as if someone had just handed me the keys to the universe.

The steady beat of the mokugyo continued to set the pace of the chant. The sharp ring of the inkin punctuated the spoken verses.

> *"O Shariputra, all dharmas are forms of Emptiness; not born, not destroyed, not stained, not pure, without loss,*

*without gain. In Emptiness, there is no form, no
sensation, perception, volitional formations,
consciousness; no eye, ear, nose, tongue, body, mind; no
color, sound, smell, taste, touch, phenomena; no realm
of sight, no realm of consciousness; no ignorance and no
end to ignorance; no old age and death, and no end to
old age and death; no suffering, no cause of suffering,
no extinguishing, no path;
no wisdom and no attainment.
No attainment and thus the Bodhisattva lives
Prajñāpāramitā, with no hindrance in the mind, no
hindrance, therefore, no fear, far beyond deluded
thoughts, this is Nirvana.*

*All past, present, and future Buddhas live
Prajñāpāramitā, and, therefore, realize unexcelled
complete Enlightenment. ... "*

I had no clue what the words "Dharma, *Prajñāpāramitā*, unexcelled complete Enlightenment" meant. It didn't matter. It was, as if, the essence of the thought; the idea presented, was much more than the words could express. It was like trying to capture a fast-flowing stream in a water glass. The ideas flowed around the words, through the words, beyond the words, and resonated their understanding in wordless places.

*"Therefore know, Prajñāpāramitā is the great mantra,
the vivid mantra, the best mantra, the unsurpassable
mantra; it ends all pain. This is the truth, not a lie. So
set forth the Prajñāpāramitā Mantra, set forth this
mantra and say:
Gate! Gate! Paragate! Parasamgate! Bodhi Svaha!
Prajñā Heart Sutra."*

That was more than twenty-five years ago. Nothing has changed; the *Heart Sutra* is, for me, the essence of the Buddha's teaching. It "says it; as it is."

I hope that this attempt to create another form from Emptiness is of value to you, dear reader.

- robert wydler haduch
zürich, february 2016

Editor's note: From time to time within the chapter text, you will see text set off as the block you are presently reading. This blocked text can be considered "tangential" commentary. As you will read, it is usually an attempt to explain a point by using an example unrelated to the text at hand. You can skip it if you like. Although, it does usually add a bit of color to the narrative.

1

BODHISATTVA AVALOKITESHVARA

Avalokiteshvara, watched, through half-opened eyes, the sun as it made its morning debut in the East. Shimmering in various shades of orange, it seemed alive as it slowly rose above the horizon. It was a wondrous sight, and it was always new, and Avalokiteshvara never tired of being a part of it.

He had sat, as was his custom, in meditation, throughout the night. Last night he and a fellow monk, Shariputra by name, had found a small grassed clearing near some temple trees that were in bloom. The heady smell of the exotic blossoms and the lightly pungent smell of the dried grasses, he had gathered together for a seating place against the cold dampness of the earth, had kept him company during the early part of the night, but not for long. He had soon drifted into a deep meditative state unaware of the waning moon that illuminated the unclouded heavens.

Soon the warming sun would reach the clearing where he was sitting and begin to burn away the heavy dew that had covered everything, including himself, in the course of the night. But for the time being, he could still sit in the dewiness and enjoy the smell of the grasses, the blossoms and of the earth around him. Licking his lips, still damp with dew, brought the flavor of the temple tree flowers to his taste buds. Fragrance and taste were inseparable; each was the other. He was thankful for the protection of his thick patchwork robe. It had kept him warm and dry throughout what seemed to have been a very short night. He smiled inwardly and thanked the Buddha for his teaching of the "middle way."

> The Buddha would often say to his disciples: "Everything in moderation. Stay on the path that courses between the extremes of self-indulgence and self-mortification. Remain alert, it is very easy to stray from the path."

The Bodhisattva knew from personal experience how uncomfortable it could be sitting in the cold, wet night without proper attire only to satisfy the desire for self-mortification.

There seemed to be something different about this morning and although he was no longer in the habit of comparing "today" with "yesterday" — something was not the same. It was just a feeling, not yet fully formed, not constrained by comparison. It was as if something that was always there was more there than ever before. It seemed to be quieter, more still than other mornings. It had to be an inner stillness because all around him the sound of nature waking to the new day was in full swing. The Falcons were "talking" back and forth to each other; as they circled high above the grassy field searching for breakfast. The land creatures they were searching for could be heard scurrying through the tall grass to the safety of their underground nests. Two melodies in counterpoint to each other and the myriad other counterpoints. By all outward signs it was an average north Indian winter morning, he reflected. And yet… not so typical, he thought. He dismissed the observation, knowing that if the night had anything special to offer, the insights would develop over the course of the day. There was no point in trying to make things happen. "Stay out of it," he told himself, with mock sternness, as he became absorbed in observing a small spider dropping on its single silken thread from the tip of a nearby stalk of barley grass. The spider descended very slowly producing the silk along the way and then, all of a sudden, it made a huge drop, of at least twenty centimeters, and disappeared from sight. The silken thread was still there, moving ever so slightly in the warming morning air, but the spider had vanished. How interesting.

The Bodhisattva, smiling at the teaching the little spider had demonstrated to him, decided it was time to meet the morning and answer the call of nature and the call of a rumbling stomach. Slowly he came out of the lotus-posture he had assumed last night, stretched his legs and slipped into sandals that had also been shielded from the heavy dew by the orange robe that he was wearing. Turning his head to the left, he noticed that Shariputra, seated some five meters away, was also stirring. They nodded a morning greeting to each other which was the equivalent of saying "Namaste, I hope your night went well. We will be meeting each other for breakfast shortly." With the greeting tendered the Bodhisattva stood up, slipped off the thick robe and shook it vigorously to remove the remaining dew, dust and any of the little creatures of the night that may have found their way into it. He then folded it neatly and laid it atop the small store of provisions that would soon become breakfast. That done he retired to the nearby thicket with its noisily gurgling stream to take care of bodily needs.

Water always amazed him. There was a magic to it. It always seemed to get to where it was going. No matter how long it took and no matter how many detours it had to make; it always got to where it was supposed to be. It was, at once, single-minded and yet totally flexible. It took the shape of where it was at the moment it was there. It took on the nature of the ambient conditions. At times it was invisible, at times it was a liquid and at times it was a solid, but it was always water. It was available for everyone and everything, and yet it was still itself. He watched as a leaf floated by going from somewhere to somewhere and the gurgling stream just carried it along seemingly without notice. He observed a low-hanging branch from a nearby shrub disturb the watery flow causing it to become roiled. But the water stream was agitated for only a moment and then it re-assumed its flow, its self. A stone, large enough to protrude out of the moving stream was not a cause for concern. The water flowed around the stone in a continually moving embrace with only a gurgle and some bubbles to mark the encounter. He scooped up some of the liquid from the stream, avoiding the leaves and other commuters on its surface and splashed his face with it. The reverie was over. He was back in this moment of time — wet and refreshed. Now it was time for breakfast.

2

SHARIPUTRA

For Shariputra, the all-night meditation had been punctuated by periods of sleep. He was quite tired from his travels. He had journeyed far and wide this year preaching and teaching the Dharma to lay people and to small gatherings of Buddhist monks. And now he, like so many other monks, was returning to a permanent place of residence for the duration of the monsoon season. There he would meet the Buddha again. They had been apart for the better part of a year and Shariputra missed him very much.

Shariputra recalled how nearly thirty years ago he had, by chance, met one of the Buddha's earliest disciples, the Venerable Assaji. Shariputra had introduced himself and asked the monk who he was. Assaji explained that he was a disciple of a teacher called Shakyamuni Buddha. Shariputra asked him: "What does the Buddha teach?" Assaji replied: "The Buddha teaches that all things in this world are impermanent. All things in this world are conditional. They arise and recede according to causes and conditions." Then Assaji went on to tell Shariputra about the Enlightened One's first sermon where he, Assaji, and four others were present. He told him how the Buddha had taught them about *The Four Noble Truths* and *The Noble Eightfold Path*. Shariputra remembered how overjoyed he was to hear these words. He was immediately enveloped in a sense of total, unqualified, unconditional understanding. He remembered thinking: "This must be the way a master bell-ringer feels being totally immersed in the sound and reverberation of a huge temple bell just struck." He remembered how his close friend Mogallana had burst into tears on hearing what Assaji had said. "Yes, that is how it began.", he said, half aloud, in answer to his memory of how he and Mogallana had left the very next day to join the Buddha's growing family of disciples at the Venuvana bamboo-grove.

Much had taken place in the thirty years since that "chance" meeting with Assaji. It was now generally acknowledged by the Buddha's sangha that Sharipurta and his friend Mogallana were the closest male disciples of the Buddha. In fact, the Buddha himself, when he was staying in Savatthi at Jeta's Grove declared Sharipurta to be his "spiritual son."

"Yes, it was very generous of the Lord to call me his *spiritual son*," thought Sharipurta. However, being the Master's *spiritual son* did not make the task of living the Dharma any easier, he thought. As the Buddha had said so many times, *understanding* is something that one has to achieve for one's self. And *achieving* does not come just because one is someone's *spiritual son*.

Sharipurta had also spent some time last night thinking about his most recent "chance" meeting. It had taken place yesterday; while he was making his way through the nearby village; knocking on doors and asking the townsfolk for something for his supper. Just ahead of him; he had spied another saffron-robed monk knocking on doors and asking for food donations. Thinking that he recognized the man's physical demeanor; he quickly caught up with him and called out a greeting. The salutation was acknowledged and it came to pass that the men knew about each other, but had never met each other. They seemed to be quite compatible and had immediately agreed to do their begging together and to share whatever came their way. And so it came to pass that the two of them found their way to the temple tree grove. There, they had lit a small fire to cook the food gifts and to warm themselves. They ate mostly in silence, savoring the cardamon flavored boiled rice and the freshly cooked root vegetables. After eating they talked for awhile, nothing of substance, and then retired to their respective "sitting places."

Shariputra was aware that the monk he had shared this evening meal with was the Bodhisattva Avalokiteshvara. He may also have been aware that Avalokiteshvara was one of eight Bodhisattva disciples of the Buddha. Shariputra had been present on some occasions when Avalokiteshvara participated as the leader of discussion groups discussing the Buddha's teachings. In many ways, the Bodhisattva was Buddha Shakyamuni's "main-man."

Shariputra would also have been aware of the meaning of Avalokiteshvara's name as "the lord who sees the sufferings of sentient beings." "Avalokita" meaning "one who looks down." "Ishvara" is changed to "eshvara" to be grammatically correct. It means "lord" or "master." "The lord who sees the sufferings of sentient beings." or "he who is the essence of compassion."

"Had the Buddha arranged this meeting between himself and Avalokiteshvara? Had the Buddha seen the suffering, doubt and confusion of Shariputra? How often does one have a 'chance' meeting with a Bodhisattva? How often is that Bodhisattva called Avalokiteshvara?", Shariputra had asked himself many times during the night.

Mentally and physically exhausted, he finally decided that "things-that-seem-to-happen-by-chance should be left-to-chance-to-happen" was the only straightforward answer to the speculations running through his head. His mind seemed to become quieter after making the decision to drop the entire matter. There was a nightbird singing somewhere in the trees. He focused on the melody and it led him into silence.

> We should mention here that Shariputra would have been very familiar with the concepts surrounding the word "Bodhisattva." He knew that a Bodhisattva was a human being that was on the path to Buddhahood. He knew that The Four Noble Truths and The Noble Eightfold Path defined the path to Buddhahood. He also knew that the path to Buddhahood was not a path. He knew these things because the Buddha had said to him, "Shariputra! I predict one day you will become a Buddha by the name of Pamaprabha. You will come to this world again to save all living beings and achieve the highest state of Buddhahood." Shariputra was in himself a Bodhisattva, but you would never hear him calling himself a Bodhisattva; that is the way it is with Bodhisattvas. They aren't hung up on names or titles — meaningless words meant to impress the gullible. It is what one does and not what one is called that defines one — this is an old law.

3

THE TELLING

While Shariputra gathered kindling and bits of dried wood for the cooking of breakfast, Avalokiteshvara busied himself with the preparation of the meal itself. It was to be a simple meal of rice and cooked apples. The apples needed some attention because they were somewhat bruised and somewhat occupied by creatures intent on eating them for their breakfast. The apples were, however, sweet and firm and worth the effort of their preparation. The rice would be cooked, slowly, and when it was about finished the thinly sliced apple pieces would be added. As a final ingredient, some cow's milk would make the whole mass a bit creamier. All in all, a hearty breakfast for the two wayfarers who would soon be on the road again.

While the Bodhisattva tended the cooking rice, Shariputra had prepared their eating place under the shade of a temple tree, and he was now doing his traditional morning asanas. The smell of the cooking rice and apples awakened their sense of being hungry. It was a comfortable feeling, and it brought with it an enjoyable anticipation of what was to become a memorable breakfast.

Neither of the men had spoken much this morning, and it was to be that way through most of their breakfast time. Eating and talking seemed like a very silly thing to do. One doesn't do justice to either act. So better to be still and savor the food than to distract oneself and the other with words. Breakfast was soon over, and both men were enjoying its aftereffects much like a cat that has just finished its eating and is sitting, quietly staring into space. The monks weren't staring into space but were seemingly fixated, in their gaze, on the glowing red embers of the cooking fire. It was then, in a moment of seemingly absolute stillness that the Bodhisattva Avalokiteshvara addressed Shariputra in a clear, well-modulated voice:

"O Shariputra, form is no other than Emptiness.
Emptiness is no other than form.
Form is exactly Emptiness. Emptiness is exactly form.
The same is true for sensation, perception, volitional formations, consciousness."

The silence was palpable. Shariputra said nothing. His eyes, locked on the eyes of the Bodhisattva, asked: "Is there more to this?"

"O Shariputra, all dharmas are forms of Emptiness;
not born, not destroyed,
not stained, not pure,
without loss, without gain.
In Emptiness, there is no form,
no sensation, perception, volitional formations,
consciousness."

The Bodhisattva looked into the eyes of Shariputra and found no hindrances, no mentations, no opinions, no thought, so he continued:

"In Emptiness
there is no eye, ear, nose, tongue, body, mind.
There is no color, sound, smell, taste, touch, phenomena.
There is no realm of sight, no realm of consciousness,
no ignorance and no end to ignorance,
no old age and death and no end to old age and death,
no suffering and no cause of suffering,
no extinguishing, no path;
no wisdom and no attainment."

Shariputra said nothing; he had not moved a muscle during the Bodhisattva's narration. Thought in its myriad of forms was absent from his mind, nothing moved and yet all was in motion. The Bodhisattva sensing Shariputra's complete attention continued:

> "No attainment and thus the Bodhisattva lives Prajñāpāramitā, with no hindrance in the mind, no hindrance, therefore, no fear, far beyond deluded thoughts, this is Nirvana.
>
> All past, present, and future Buddhas live Prajñāpāramitā, and, therefore, realize unexcelled complete Enlightenment."

Neither man said anything. Both were gazing at the remains of a cooking fire; that was now reduced to embers glowing a dull red from under a powdery ash blanket.

Avalokiteshvara was, for his part, amazed at how the words had formed themselves into sentences to express the insights that were the result of the deep meditation of the previous night. He had no sense of ownership regarding the thoughts expressed in the words he had just spoken. The words were just there. They came together without his conscious intervention. He was the vehicle for their expression, but they were not his words. It was as if a puppet master, a "Sutradhar" (or "holder of strings") was speaking through him. He stopped this analysis – immediately. He knew that, in the next moment, he might find himself caught up; trying to explain to himself what had happened. The analysis was a sure way to destroy the essence of the insights. Insights that were already diluted by the words he had spoken. He moved away from the growing chatter in his mind and looked deeper into the dying fire.

Shariputra was still in a non-word, non-thought state. He did not try to capture, or try to remember, or try to catalog, or try to compare what he had just heard. He was not making any decisions, forming any opinions. He was just sitting and staring into the glowing embers. It was as if a huge wave had flowed over him; he still felt submerged in it — offering no resistance. Of course, it was only later that these sensations became his thoughts. For the time being all was still.

It may have been the song of the oxcart driver or the sound of the oxcart bumping along the dirt road on its way to somewhere that put an end to the profound quiet that had surrounded the two men. They looked out in the direction of the oxcart and then looked to each other and bowed their heads to one another simultaneously. It was over. Each man stood up and stretched.

Shariputra began cleaning the eating utensils. He took the cooking pots to the stream, washed them and then placed them in the sun to dry. He would pack them before they left this place and then secure them safely in a nearby hollowed log ready for other wayfarers to use when staying at the temple tree grove.

The Bodhisattva doused the remaining embers with a good measure of water and with the same resolve that he had doused the speculations that had tried to dilute the previous night's insights. "Yes, an open fire and speculations have a lot in common. One shouldn't leave either of them unattended," he ruminated. He then reminded himself that there was one more thing he needed to tell Shariputra; even though the Bodhisattva surmised that Shariputra would be already well aware of what he would say to him.

4

WORDS ARE SURROGATES

Our story of the meeting of Shariputra and the Bodhisattva Avalokiteshvara ends here. Did it happen this way? Could it have happened this way? Was there a conversation between the two monks that was then transcribed by one of them, or by a third person, and then later titled the *Heart Sutra*? Could it have been a conversation in the mind realm and not the physical realm? Was the conversation a convenient literary vehicle designed to support the words uttered by the Bodhisattva? Any explanation we propose to answer these questions would be rife with speculation.

What we do know is that no one is quite sure of how, or when, or where the *Heart Sutra* came into existence. But it is here for us to do with it what we wish. We can chant it in Sanskrit, Chinese, Japanese, English or a host of other languages. We can choose to believe in or to not-believe in the words. We can speculate on the meaning of the phrases. We can apply all of our intellectual efforts to further our intellectual understanding of it. We can write books about it. We can do all of these things. But at some point in time, we have to stop with these approaches if we wish to get to the essence of the *Heart Sutra*.

I think this is what the Bodhisattva Avalokiteshvara had reminded himself to tell Shariputra. He had reminded himself to tell Shariputra that his words were only a description of a state of being. A state of being where:

"...form is no other than Emptiness.
Emptiness is no other than form.
Form is exactly Emptiness. Emptiness is exactly form.

> *The same is true for sensation, perception, volitional formations, consciousness."*

The Bodhisattva was using *words* to describe a *non-word* state. Words are a product of our thought. Our thought is a product of our memories. Our memories are recordings of the past. Everything in memory is history, "yesterday's news."

We all have had moments in our lives when we have tried to relate certain moments to ourselves or others using words, and we found it to be virtually impossible to do.

> You have fallen in love for the first time in your life. Please describe this experience in 50 words or less. Except for articles, conjunctions or prepositions **do not** repeat any of the words in your description of the experience. Read what you have just written. Are you truly satisfied that you have fully described the experience?

Maybe Avalokiteshvara would have said it something like this: "Look Shariputra, what I have told you is just a description of my experience. This verbal description is fraught with danger for any number of reasons. For example, I have used words that are familiar to me. These words may not be familiar to you and even if the words are familiar to you, you may define them differently. Then again you may not have heard everything that I have said because of a stray thought entering your mind. There are many other dangers that we could both enumerate. But I think we both understand that if you accept and believe what I say without proving it for yourself, without experiencing it for yourself, you will not have understood what I have said to you."

> You sit down at a table in a restaurant; the waiter brings you a menu card. You are famished. You look at the various offerings. You recognise some of them from previous eating

experiences. You devour the words and intellectually savor the promises of the written word. You may even ask the waiter to explain to you what some of the entrées promise to be. After a time, you push the menu away, pick up the napkin and wipe your lips, let out a intellectually satisfying burp, get up from the table and without leaving a tip, you walk out of the restaurant. You have now had the intellectual experience of eating lunch. Were you satisfied? Ask your stomach.

5

Prajñāpāramitā

"The Bodhisattva Avalokiteshvara actively engaged in Prajñāpāramitā,…"

The opening lines of the *Heart Sutra* tell us that the Bodhisattva was in profound meditation. We can safely assume that he had comfortably seated himself in a quiet place; body erect and at ease; breathing in a regular rhythm, not forced; eyes unfocused; hands in some manner of mudra; fully awake; doing nothing. He may have had brought his attention, gently to focus, to his breath; thereby, helping to eliminate thoughts by non-attending to them. He may have brought his attention, gently to focus, on what was passing through his mind – a passive awareness. Passive, meaning he had no mental reaction to what was passing through his mind. He was not making decisions, formulating opinions, adding to the chain of thought, creating stories, creating worries, massaging his ego. No, he was just in the stream of sensory inputs without forming opinions about them. And because he was not producing thoughts about these inputs, they no longer influenced his being. And the thoughts dropped away. However, this was only the beginning. He had just "stepped into the stream" as the old saying goes.

Avalokiteshvara went on to realize the state that some call *Prajñāpāramitā,* the "Perfection of Transcendent Wisdom." In other words, "perfected Wisdom" that is "beyond the limits of all possible experience and knowledge."

When is one beyond "the limits of all possible experience?" When is one beyond "the limits of all possible knowledge?" What is *experience*? What is *knowledge*?

Here are some common synonyms for the word *experience* when used as a noun: cognitive content, happening, mental object, natural event, occurrence. It is easy to make the case that all of these words have something to do with *thought*.

Here are some common synonyms for the word *knowledge* when used as a noun: awareness, consciousness, realization, recognition, cognition, apprehension, perception, appreciation of something. It is easy to make the case that all of these words have something to do with *thought*.

If the Bodhisattva was "beyond the limits of all possible experience and knowledge," he was beyond the boundaries of thought and therefore beyond the boundaries of words. If something is beyond the confines of thought and word is there a way of communicating this something to another? What a dilemma, trying to describe a state that exists beyond the realm of words using words – impossible. The *Perfection of Transcendent Wisdom* – no more experience, no more knowledge, beyond thought and word. It is not something that one can verbalize. It must be self-realized. We can call it *Prajñāpāramitā*, but the word is not the thing. The word cat is not a cat and the word *Prajñāpāramitā* is not *Prajñāpāramitā*. Can we realize this state, which is "beyond the limits of all possible experience and knowledge?"

6

CAN WE REALIZE PRAJÑĀPĀRAMITĀ?

> You are sitting in a train, looking out of the window at the passing countryside. The landscape flows by in a never-ending stream. You are aware of the moving stream, but you are not actively involved in thinking about it or anything else. You are not naming it or making stories about it in your mind. "Oh, look at that black cat in the field. Is it hunting? Is it waiting for a friend? Is it this? Is it that?" No, none of that. No speculations, no naming. The cat was there, and now it is not there. Was it even a cat?
>
> It begins in the moment, and it ends in the moment. There is no holding on to a mental afterimage. It is an awareness that is passive — no naming; no residuals; no kicking up the dust of memory; no cause and effect; no karma creation; no karma reinforcement.

You can try this experiment for yourself. You can see how the mind becomes very still if you do not interact with the sensory inputs streaming through the train window. You know that you are not in a hypnotized state. You can move in and out of this state by creating a thought, by recognizing an object or responding to some other sensory input — for example "tickets, please." You can then move back into this passive state. At the start, you may find it to be difficult; but as you become more passively attentive to what is going on around you; it becomes largely automatic. After all, does every passing sight, sound, smell, touch need your immediate attention, or opinion, or comment, or:

We can assume that we have the innate ability to experience "...*form is no other than Emptiness. Emptiness is no other than form.*" We can also expect that this experience may not be immediately forthcoming. As someone once said: "*A journey of a thousand miles begins with a single step.*"

And as with any journey that one undertakes; it will require a good measure of trial and error, patience, courage and common sense. It is not magic. It doesn't need a guru. It is not a team effort. It is something one must do alone.

Where does one begin? One begins exactly where one is at this very moment. How does one begin? One begins by paying attention to what one is doing at this very moment. One has to jump into the river with both feet. The attitude: "I'll start later; I'm too busy right now." leads to nowhere. One knows that. One has used this excuse or a similar version of it many times before, and one is now exactly where one was then – nowhere, absolutely nowhere. Why does one torture oneself with these promises that one never seems to fulfill? Who is one satisfying? Why?

> What are you attending to this very moment? How deeply are you engaged in the reading of this text? What are you thinking about at this very instant? Do you know? Are you worrying about something? Are you planning something? Are you stewing in anger about something? Who or what are you hating this very moment? What opinions are you forming about this book? What else are you doing while you are "pretending" to read this text? Are you alert? Are you eating something? Are you listening to music? Are you talking to someone? Are you petting your cat? Are you texting one of your 2000+ friends on social media?

We lead lives so full of distractions that we are totally oblivious to our being totally distracted. We assume this is the way the world turns. We regard our colleagues and find that they are running just as fast as we are. Our comrades look at us and worry that we are running just as fast as they are. We whirl in this whirlwind; this perpetual motion machine sustained by trite little soundbites like "time is money", "greed is good", "you are either with us, or you are against us." We are like a 10,000 piece jigsaw puzzle still in the box, fragmented, disconnected, topsy-turvy. Our minds respond to every stimulus that promises success and satisfaction. Our minds are so busy attending to everything around us, real and imagined, that we have forgotten what it is like to be quiet. Were we ever quiet?

Isn't it time to open the puzzle box and to peek inside? Isn't it time to look at who we truly are?

7

OPEN THE PUZZLE BOX

Opening the puzzle box for the first time should be done somewhere where one feels sheltered from the barrage of distractions that make up one's ordinary daily existence. Find a quiet place away from people and things. Tell your "significant other" that you are going to sit, quietly, by yourself. Sit in a chair or on the floor. Make yourself comfortable. There are no rules or methods, but there are a couple of hints one should consider.

One must remember that one has, in a sense, pulled oneself off of the daily merry-go-round when one attempts to "sit in silence." We each have our version of this merry-go-round. We call it "our life." Getting off of this merry-go-round can be very fearful for some that define themselves in terms of other people's opinions, or things, or titles, or careers, etc. We all know people that are completely caught up in their process of "becoming" someone or something. They are totally unaware that the only thing they are becoming is befuddled. A sad affair, indeed, but a common one today in our monoculture society. As J. Krishnamurti once said, *"It is no measure of health to be well adjusted to a profoundly sick society."* And yet that is what we spend most of our time in this life doing — adjusting to a society that is profoundly sick.

The thing one must remember is that many people have abandoned their out of control merry-go-round and the illusion of "getting somewhere" or "being someone or something." It is doable, but it requires a quietness of mind that is not allowed to anyone that rides the ersatz horses on the carousel.

A truly quiet mind is a rare commodity. One finds that out very quickly when one first begins to sit in so-called "meditation." A noisy mind and a fidgety body are a normal state of affairs that confronts anyone at the beginning of an attempt to "sit in silence." It is not a reason to stop one's sitting-in-silence, one's meditation sessions. It is a reason to re-dedicate oneself to continuing with what one has begun.

In our everyday interaction with this world, the mind is kept quite busy dealing with situations real and imagined. A typical day involves the mind in any number of factual pursuits and fanciful pursuits. One can observe this for oneself by just watching what one is doing, saying or thinking during the day. The mind is busy, busy, busy and most of its busyness has to do with the maintenance of one's "self." One can observe this fact quite readily but whether one accepts this observation as factual is another matter. One is, so to say, in a perpetual "selfie mode" snapping mental images of one's self and then continuously correcting or "photoshopping" the resulting image so that it meets or exceeds a mental image of today's "ideal me."

Maintaining these feedback loops demands much time and energy. And it is not only our personal energy but the energy of everyone we have contact with in the course of the day. We all know people that are constantly vying for "center-stage." We all know how these "high-maintenance" individuals can make our lives miserable. Fortunately, we are not in that category.

> You are walking through a shopping mall or anywhere where there are large display windows. Count the times you give a sideward glance at the reflecting window surface to observe yourself. Count the times you look directly into the window; not to observe what is in the display window but to see your reflected image. While you are looking at yourself, pay atten-

tion to the thoughts that are going through your mind. "Oh, I must lose a bit of weight. Oh, my hair is such a mess. Oh, this. Oh, that." Amazing isn't it? Now, just for the fun of it, count the times you observe other walkers-by sideward glancing into the display windows. What are they talking about to themselves?

One of the first things that one discovers when one begins to explore "sitting still" is that the body may not know how to sit still. One discovers this by observing the body as it "sits." Mentally scanning the body on a regular basis, with an attentive mind, is usually enough to eliminate the body's unconscious jerks and twitches. One may find that, over the years, one has accumulated some habits that now one finds to be embarrassing. Therefore, one must conduct the mental scan without recrimination. There is no one to fault. And if there were, who would it be? A regular, rhythmic breath is an amazingly efficient body and mind silencer, and it doesn't have any negative aftereffects.

If the sitting position one initially assumes when seeking silence becomes painful, one changes it. If one loses one's breath, or if it becomes intermittent, or shallow, or otherwise burdensome, one changes it. One pays attention to what is going on in the body and the mind. Sooner or later, if one is consistent; one will find a comfortable way of sitting; whether it be cross-legged on the floor, or on a bench, or in a chair. It doesn't matter; if one sits in full or partial lotus. The idea is to sit comfortably. It is not a gymnastic exercise. Forget the fancy mudras. Let your hands come together naturally in your lap. Never mind the mantras and invocations. The idea is to quiet the mind rather than fill it with other distractions. What matters is that one is not fighting the breath or the body. Common sense should prevail. A comfortable sitting position contributes to quieting the mind. A quiet mind contributes to a comfortable sitting position.

As the body quiets down, our consciousness of it becomes vague because it is no longer sending signals of discomfort to the brain. The body signals, the internal signals, are replaced, in our attention, by external signals. These external signals have always been there. The internal signals had, previously, a higher priority in our attention. These external signals now dominate our consciousness. Every sound, every odor, every vibration, every sight is now, seemingly, magnified. Sounds one would have never heard in the usual helter-skelter of the day are now "boom-box"-ing in one's brain. One tries to recognise, to identify, these sounds. One tries to block them out. After all, if one does not block them out how can one sit in silence? The eyes, peering intently on the carpeted floor, see every carpet strand, every bit of carpet grime the vacuum cleaner did not pick up. Should one count the carpet strands or the carpet dirt? One's thoughts are sense bound. One is caught in the sense world. One is juggling six disparate signal sources at the same time, or in a linear fashion, or… is one losing one's mind?

No, one is not losing one's mind. One is discovering one's mind. One is, maybe for the first time in one's life, seeing the form of one's day-to-day mind. All of the senses are sending their signals to the brain, just as they have always done. That hasn't changed. What has changed is that one has become more conscious of these signals because one is less aware of a physical body that is now sitting in comfort.

The question becomes, "Is it the vibration one is sensing that is destroying the silence or is it one's thoughts about the vibration that is holding the silence in abeyance? Is it the light pattern one sees keeping the silence at bay or is it one's thoughts about the light pattern that is the culprit?" When one begins to ask oneself questions such as these one begins to discover the type of mind game that one plays —

all of the time. We create our noise – all of the time. We call this noise – thinking.

Why is it important for one to identify with the sounds that reach one's ears? Why is it important to us to categorize, to name, these sound vibrations? The noise of the oncoming freight train is not a danger signal unless one is sitting on the rails. Is it necessary to engage the noise in a mental conversation when one is not sitting on the tracks? "Oh, that train is too loud. Oh, I enjoy the 'clickety-clack' sound of the wheels." Who or what is being served in this mind-game?

Why is it important to know that the vacuum cleaner or the person using it did not do a thorough job in cleaning the carpet? Why? Why bother with these thoughts, these speculations? Why do we carry on these nonsensical conversations with ourselves – continuously?

Once one becomes aware that the senses are only the source of the signal and that they are not the source of the mental noise, one's being becomes automatically quieter. One does not try to or need to block out the sensory inputs; this is never a successful strategy because it involves thinking. Thinking creates the noise. If one does not respond to the sense inputs with thought, in time, sight and sound and smell, etc. fall away. They seemingly disappear because the thoughts associated with the them have fallen away. Does this mean that one is in a helpless trance? Does this mean that if the sputtering candle on the tabletop, for some reason, sets fire to the curtain that is in its vicinity, one will not respond to the danger? No, to both questions. One is not asleep when thought deserts the mind. One is more awake than one has ever been before. One will only "see" that in retrospect and not while one is "out-of-thought."

And what one "sees" is a thoroughly refreshed mind. You will know it when you experience it. Do not go looking for this state. You will not find it. You will be looking for it with thought. We have already concluded that thought is the problem and not the solution. Just be present where-you-are when you-are-there.

Every Buddha, every Bodhisattva, at some time or another, has gone through the same trials and tribulations one is going through now. It is a matter of staying true to oneself no matter how many lifetimes it may take. After all, what else of lasting value, is there to do in this life?

8

Good News

"The Bodhisattva Avalokiteshvara actively engaged in Prajñāpāramitā, clearly saw the Five Skandhas to be empty, thus completely overcoming Ignorance."

The Bodhisattva Avalokiteshvara; actively engaged in *Prajñāpāramitā*; fully awake; not in a trance state; not asleep; beyond the reach of thought; experienced the profound meditative state where form, sensation, perception, volitional formations and consciousness (i.e. the *Five Skandhas*) are seen to have no underlying sub-stance. He "*clearly saw the Five Skandhas to be empty.*"

When we say "*clearly saw the Five Skandhas to be empty,*" we do not deny the existence of the *Five Skandhas*. We are stating they exist only because of something else existing. They have no self-substance in the same way that "empty promises" and "empty words" are empty.

This genuine understanding, this experience of insight, distilled into word, became the text of the *Heart Sutra*.

We too, from time to time, experience genuine understanding. We, in a rare moment, see something for what it truly is. This "seeing" is a state of no doubting, no "opinionating" and no waffling between this, that or something else. It is a feeling, a deep seemingly sourceless feeling, a "gut feeling" if you will. We all have these momentary experiences if we are at all conscious. We usually destroy them because we "think them to death" by trying to analyze them. Or we lose them because we are busy congratulating ourselves on how clever we were to see something as it truly was. Our mistake is to take the experience and put it into a thought form. When we do that, we clothe it in our personal image, our personal bias. And it no longer exists as an insight, something original, something new; it exists as yesterday's news because we are, in a sense, yesterday's news. We always work in the past because we rely on thought and thought is founded in memory and memory is the past.

The response to an experience of insight is *action*. *Action* is spontaneous. *Action* is selfless. *Action* is not a result of thought, of thinking. Re-*action* is a result of thought, of thinking. We are usually in re-*action* mode. We respond to the present moment with thought. Our *action* is then based on this thought (or thoughts). That is why it is called a re-*action*. This process takes time. Our response, no matter how quickly it comes, is always too late. It is not spontaneous. We are using the memory of a previous experience (with variations) to deal with the immediate moment. We are always "a day late and a dollar short" as the old saying goes. We experience suffering and affliction because we are not in tune with the moment. We are in the state of *Dukkha*.

> Our normal approach to the moment at hand is a lot like a movie where the sound is not in synch with the images, or it is like a dancer that is out of synch with the music. Painful!

When the Bodhisattva completely overcame ignorance, he completely overcame suffering and affliction. When he understood that the *Five Skandhas* were empty, he understood that suffering and affliction were empty. He didn't think about it; it was evident. It was in plain sight. Does this mean that suffering and affliction do not exist in this life? No, it means that we do not properly understand how and why they exist.

The opening lines of the *Heart Sutra* are a confirmation, in no uncertain terms, of the core teaching of the Buddha. The Bodhisattva "*clearly saw the Five Skandhas to be empty.*" We, as humans, as Bodhisattvas-to-be-yet-awakened, should also be able to discover that the *Five Skandhas* are empty. What is it that keeps us in the dark? What will it take before we – clearly see the *Five Skandhas* for ourselves?

Of course, before we can clearly see the *Five Skandhas* to be empty, we should have an understanding of what these concepts attempt to convey. To do that, we must leave the *Heart Sutra* text and talk a bit about *The Four Noble Truths* and *The Noble Eightfold Path*. But before we do that, we will spend some time talking about Siddhārtha Gautama, the historical Buddha. It was he that formulated *The Four Noble Truths* and *The Noble Eightfold Path* as a result of his Enlightenment while sitting under the bodhi tree.

9

THE SOON-TO-BE-BUDDHA

Siddhārtha did not spend much time bathing in the pool. He stayed only long enough to wash off the dust of the morning journey. He and Channa, his favorite servant, had for the fourth time this week made their way into Kapilavastu and the surrounding territory without the knowledge of King Suddhodhana, Siddhārtha's father.

> The Prince was not allowed out of the royal compound without a royal entourage, and not before the roads, and the town had been swept clean of all signs of human misery and sorrow. Whenever the Prince was traveling, the king's servants made sure he would not see anyone that was sick, or old, or dying or begging. This charade had begun some twenty-nine years before, when the king, not a tyrant to his people, had learned from his teacher, the Sage Asitha, and his Brahmin advisors that his newly born son was destined to become a Buddha. The king, initially overjoyed at the news, soon became unhappy because he surmised that, if Siddhārtha were to become a Buddha, he could not be king of the Shakya clan. Over the ensuing years, the King did everything he could to ensure that Siddhārtha would choose the way of kinghood and not the path to Buddhahood. Siddhārtha enjoyed the best of everything and all in good measure. The prince had become involved in the duties of his royal status. He had proven himself to the tribe elders that he was exceptionally intelligent and also an excellent warrior. He had married well and his wife, Yashodharā, had borne him a son, Rāhula.
>
> It was a grand charade, and it seemed to be working. The prince was a captive, albeit a voluntary, unknowing prisoner in the human dream. It was probably not much different than the personal vision we are caught in, of course at a much less "royal" level.
>
> The dream began falling apart when Siddhārtha was twenty-nine years old.

Siddhārtha, after his bath, wandered into the garden. The flowers waving in the morning breeze painted the air with their exotic scents. The songbirds were in full soprano chorus while the buzzing bees supplied the bass. The bubbling fountains added a bit of a percussion. Vivid colors were everywhere, changing, moving. Light and shadow, shadow and light, danced with the colors. It was a heady, exotic experience when one's senses were fully engaged, and usually, Siddhārtha was fully involved. This morning, however, things were a bit different. The prince was deep in thought. The prince was deeply troubled. He had discovered on his journeys with Channa that the world outside the royal compound was not the same as the world inside the royal compound. He had seen sickness, old age, death, and also an ascetic walking in the town. Siddhārtha had seen the human condition for what it truly was. He had seen sorrow and grief, pain and suffering. He had seen things that had, so far, been absent from his life. On these journeys with Channa, he learned what his future was to be. He understood that in time, he would grow old; become ill, and he would die. And he asked himself; "Why does humanity suffer in this fashion? What is the cause of this cycle of birth, sickness, old age, and death?" And when he thought about the ascetic he had seen in the street, he asked himself; "Why can I not be like this man and search for the answer to these questions myself?"

Siddhārtha's mind whirled in the whirlpool of these thoughts. The garden had disappeared. His world was collapsing. Things that he had considered significant only hours ago no longer seemed to have any substance. In the distance, he heard his son laughing while at play with his mother Yashodharā and her maidservants. It was as if it were taking place in another dream, another world, in which he was a stranger. A tear came to his eye. He would not hear that sound of laughter for much longer. He would soon be leaving this paradise. He had to find the answer to the question of life and death. It was no longer a matter of choice. It had been foretold. And now the foretelling was to be actualized.

The day passed, evening came and went, and the prince did not sleep. He roamed the palace grounds. He walked through the various public rooms of the palace. He wandered into the stables and talked with the horses. He took some water from the fountain. He had not eaten much during the day, but he was not hungry. The moon and the stars kept him company. Every now and again a shooting star lit the dark sky as if to brighten his mood. He came to peace with himself. His resolve to answer the question of life and death was stronger now than it had been earlier in the day. He would talk to his father and Yashodharā come morning and by evening time, he would be gone. He spent the remaining hours of the warm night asleep in the garden wrapped in his cloak. A foretaste of his new life.

The following day was spent making arrangements for his leaving. He spoke to his father, his wife and his close associates about his plans to lead a life as an ascetic and to realize his call to the religious life. Needless to say, no one was happy about his decision. Many of his companions could not understand how he could throw away an earthly kingdom for what seemed to be nothing more than a whim, in their eyes.

Siddhārtha left that night leaving behind all the trappings of royalty. He traded his rich attire for a simple robe, cut off his long hair, packed his begging bowls, found a suitable walking staff, put on some sturdy sandals and was gone.

10

SIX YEARS

It is written that Siddhārtha initially found his way to the hermitage where the holy Alara Kalama taught the doctrine of renunciation to a large number of disciples. One day Alara offered Siddhārtha the post of a teacher, because of Siddhārtha's excellent understanding of the dogma. After thinking over Kalama's offer, he decided that this doctrine of renunciation would not lead to deliverance. He kindly refused the offer and left the hermitage.

Siddhārtha then set out for the country of Magadha, situated in what is now west-central Bihar state in north-eastern India. There he dwelt on a mountain slope near the city of Rajagriha. He would often visit the city to beg for food; the townspeople he met thought him to be a god.

The local king, Vimbasara, went to visit Siddhārtha in his mountain retreat. The king, it is written, tried to convince Siddhārtha to give up his hermit-like existence and join him as a companion. He even offered to share his kingdom with Siddhārtha if he would join him in the city. To all these offers, Siddhārtha replied: "no thank you." And then he added the reason for his refusal. Here is what he said to the king:

> "I know the vanity of all desire. Desires are like poison; wise men despise them. I have thrown them away as one would throw away a wisp of dry straw. Desires are as perishable as the fruit of a tree. They are as wayward as the clouds in the sky. They are as treacherous as the rain. They are as changeable as the wind! Suffering is born of desire. No man has ever

gratified all his wants. But they that seek wisdom, they that ponder truth, they are the ones that find peace. Who drinks salt water increases his thirst; who flees from desire finds his appetite appeased. I no longer know desire. I seek the true law."
- *The Life of Buddha:* Andre Ferdinand Herold -1922

There was a famous hermit named Rudraka that lived in the vicinity of Rajagriha. He had many disciples. Siddhārtha also visited this man only to find that like Alara Kalama he knew nothing of the true law.

Siddhārtha soon left Magadha and with five of Rudraka's disciples he found his way to the banks of the river called Nairañjanā. It was here, near the village of Uruvela, that Siddhārtha spent six years meditating and practicing the very austere physical disciplines that, over time, reduced his body to skin and bone. It was here that Siddhārtha, one day, decided that if he kept up these austere physical practices, he would be dead before he discovered truth. He stopped the practices and began to eat the food offerings that the local villagers were very pleased to bring to him. He soon regained his strength; his body took on a semblance of normalcy. He discarded the worn out rags he was wearing and sewed himself a robe from the orange colored fabric of a dead slave's funeral shroud. He bathed, washed the garment, dried it in the sun, donned it and began searching for a place to meditate. He had discarded his life of austerity after having decided that the "middle way" made more sense. In other words, not too much of something and not too little of something, everything in balance, no desire to attain and no desire to refrain.

Observing the changes that Siddhārtha was making in his life, the five disciples left his company and went on to Benares, convinced that he had given up the quest.

Siddhārtha, for his part, crossed over the river, Nairañjanā, and entered the area of Bodh Gaya.

The Ascetic Buddha

11

THE BODHI TREE

There is a tree that stands, today, in Bodh Gaya, India, near the Mahabodhi Temple. Officially it is known as a *Ficus religiosa* or sacred fig. It is a species native to the Indian subcontinent, south-west China and Indochina. It is a beautiful creation that can live hundreds of years, grow to a height of thirty meters and a diameter of three meters. The leaves are, on average fourteen centimeters long and ten centimeters broad. They are in the shape of a heart with a distinctive "drip tip." It is interesting to note that the leaves move even when the air about them is still. There is, of course, a scientific explanation why this happens, but many people attribute it to the gods and devas that live in the branches of the tree. This tree is also known as the Bodhi tree, Pippala tree, Peepal tree or Ashwattha tree. It is considered sacred to the Jainists, Hindus and Buddhists.

It was the ancestor of the presently standing Bodhi tree that sheltered Siddhārtha that fateful day when he decided that he would sit beneath it until he reached Buddhahood.

The Buddha-soon-to-be was thirty-five years old when he began searching for a place to meditate in Bodh Gaya. Whether he was led to the tree or whether it was an accidental discovery is a matter for conjecture. The fact is, when he saw the Bodhi tree, he knew he had found his meditation place. He first went to the east of the tree and bowed seven times. He then faced the tree and bowed. Placing fresh grasses at the base of the tree in a suitable fashion for sitting, he then sat down. His back was to the tree, his face to the east. He began his meditation with a bit of pranayama (yogic breathing exercises). He then vowed that he would not get up until he had attained the Bodhi state.

When he finally did stand up again, his world, our world, this world was no longer the same.

What transpired in those hours of sitting under the sacred tree and the seven weeks that followed his Enlightenment experience is an incredible story. It has been recorded in many different sutras and texts, and we will retell it once again in the following chapters.

12

UNDER THE BODHI TREE

It is said that right from the beginning of Siddhārtha's meditation Mara was there to tempt him. Mara is, in Buddhism, the personification of all that is detrimental to the spiritual life. He is a master tempter, making the banal alluring. He and his three daughters are responsible for many a shipwrecked religious life. We all have met him and his children in one form or another during our lives. He is not only active during our periods of meditation. He can be found lurking in many places; if one is alert to his methods. Usually, we are not as successful as was Siddhārtha in overcoming Mara's allurements.

In any event, no matter what temptations Mara presented, no matter how fearsome he made himself out to be, no matter how alluring his daughters made themselves out to be, no matter how many other demons he brought to the party, it didn't work.

It is written that the following exchange took place between Mara and Siddhārtha. Mara said: "The seat of enlightenment rightfully belongs to me and not to a mortal." To which Mara's soldiers, in chorus added: "We are his witness!" Mara then continued: "These warriors speak for me. Who will speak for you?" Siddhārtha reached out his right hand to touch the earth, and the earth itself spoke: "I bear you witness!" Mara was vanquished.

Siddhārtha weathered the mental turmoil. Mara withdrew and went looking for easier prey to confuse and confound. With Mara gone, Siddhārtha was able to settle into a deeper state of meditation.

It is said that in the 1st watch of the night (6-9pm), Siddhārtha arrived at the knowledge of all that had transpired in his previous births.

In the 2nd watch of the night (9-12pm), he arrived at the knowledge of how all beings are born, sicken, grow old and die. He realized the impermanence of life. He realized how karmic effects convey a being through the *cycle of life and death* (Samsāra) over and over again. He found the power of seeing everything from all sides and distances.

In the 3rd watch, he asked himself: "*What is the cause of old age and death?*" He realized the immediate cause of old age and death to be *birth*. Then he asked: "What is the cause of *birth*?" And he realized, that there was a cause that produced the effect called *birth*. He then went further into this chain of cause and effect and he finally came to the cause known as *Ignorance*. At this point, he declared, "The cause of old age and death is *Ignorance*."

This chain of cause and effect, comprised of twelve elements, became known as the *Doctrine of Dependent Arising* or the *Doctrine of Co-Arising*. The formulation of this Doctrine, by the Buddha, is the theme of the next chapter.

When the morning sun broke over the horizon, the Bodhisattva Siddhārtha Gautama was now a Buddha. He was the "Awakened One." He had realized the enlightenment that ends the cycle of life and death.

However, it did not end there. History records that the Buddha stayed in the vicinity of the Bodhi tree for seven weeks after his enlightenment. A part of this time he devoted to formulating a way to present what he had experienced to others; so they could also free themselves from

Saṃsāra — the cycle of life and death. It is said that initially, the Buddha was not sure that his experiences could be conveyed to others in a fashion that they, not personally having had the experiences, would understand.

Eventually, after much thought and much more meditation, he formulated, among other things, *The Four Noble Truths* and *The Noble Eightfold Path*. These two bodies of concepts comprise the core teachings of the Buddha. He spent the next forty-five years of his life teaching these principles to anyone who would listen to him.

The Buddha defined *The Four Noble Truths* as follows:

> *Truth of Dukkha;*
> *Origin of Dukkha;*
> *Cessation of Dukkha;*
> *Path of Liberation from Dukkha.*

They are called "*Noble*" because they offer a radical approach to the understanding of life and death based on reason and deep meditation and not on *Revelation*.

> There is revelation, and there is *Revelation*. In this text, we are using the word *Revelation* to mean the proclamations of a Supreme Being to His creatures. These disclosures are made through and interpreted by intermediaries. These agents are the prophets and the priests that we consciously and unconsciously empower with the ability to "talk to the gods."

Revelation requires one to accept as infallible the narration of someone else's experience. Understanding based on someone else's personal experience is not understanding at all. It is *belief*.

Belief is not provable. It is not a fact. It is not a theory. It does not allow for a hypothesis. It is not experiential. It is someone's idea. For it to be accepted, it requires one to have faith. This means that one trusts what one is told as true. One mentally swallows someone's unprovable ideas. One has given someone the "keys to one's mind."

Belief requires one to accept the authority of someone or something (e.g. a book) without knowing (or caring) anything about the veracity of that someone or something. This blind acceptance means one abdicates one's own ability to understand. One does this voluntarily, and without question.

Belief requires constant maintenance and support. If one considers oneself to be a rational, thinking person one finds that many of the things *Revealed,* do not make any sense in a rational, thinking world. We are all aware of examples where belief and fact have come into conflict.

Belief in the *Revealer of Revelation* depends on one's faith in someone that vouches for the authority of the *Revealer*. The people that vouchsafe the *Revealer of Revelation* are mortal human beings. They, like each one of us, have their personal agenda. Look around you. Look at how many religions are out there today. Look at the principals who are promulgating the precepts of the various religious systems. Look at the death and destruction these belief systems have supported since the dawn of history. And now look at yourself as a believer; is this who you are? Isn't it time to walk away from this bit of ignorance?

One is not asked, cajoled, threatened or otherwise put under any pressure to believe what the Buddha taught. To paraphrase the last words of the Buddha to Ananda and the assembled Sangha:
> "You are the Light itself.
> Rely on yourself,

Do not rely on others."
-taken from the *Atta Dipa*

How does one do that? How does one become *a light onto oneself?* One does that by understanding *The Four Noble Truths*:

Truth of Dukkha;
Origin of Dukkha;
Cessation of Dukkha;
Path of Liberation from Dukkha.

The *Path of Liberation from Dukkha*, the *Fourth Noble Truth*, is known as *The Noble Eightfold Path*.

The Noble Eightfold Path is defined as:
Right View,
Right Intentions,
Right Speech,
Right Action,
Right Livelihood,
Right Effort,
Right Mindfulness,
Right Meditation.

It all fits together logically, reasonably, skillfully. No smoke and mirrors, no rabbit out of a hat, no belief, no hope, no faith — only courage.

13

DOCTRINE OF DEPENDENT ARISING
or the Doctrine of Co-Arising

It is written that when Ananda, the Buddha's attendant, first heard the *Doctrine of Dependent Arising,* he said something to the effect that "The whole thing seemed quite evident to him." The Buddha rebuked him saying: "Ananda, do not talk like that. In fact, the teaching is quite profound." That should be fair warning to us; this matter of *Dependent Arising* is more than just idle thought.

We begin our mental journey into this Doctrine by saying that this is not a theory constructed by the Buddha. The *Doctrine of Dependent Arising* is a result of the profound insights the Buddha brought back from *Prajñāpāramitā* (The state that is known as *Perfection of Transcendent Wisdom.* The state that is beyond the limits of all possible experience and knowledge.)

The *Doctrine of Dependent Arising* is best defined as a description of the transience and interdependence of all things that manifest in this world:

> "This being, that becomes;
> from the arising of this, that arises;
> this not being, that does not become;
> from the ceasing of this, that ceases."

This is "the wheel of life."
This is Samsāra.
This is our past existence.
This is our present existence.
This is our future re-birth.
This is all there is as long as
we persist to exist in
Ignorance.
The Buddha, it is said,
traversed this loop of cause
and effect in both directions
and found the relationships
to be true.

Let us now go through the twelve steps of the *Doctrine of Dependent Arising*. It is said that the Buddha asked himself a series of questions on Enlightenment night. Each succeeding question was the result of the answer to the previous question. He, in that way, discovered the chain of cause and effect. But again, we should be very cautious and not expect this chain to be totally linear in its unfolding. Some items "fold-back" on each other. They support each other in both directions, clockwise and counter-clockwise. We can look at this chain like a bicycle chain. It is a continuous loop. If we travel the chain in the clockwise direction, we begin with *Ignorance* and end with *Old Age & Death*. If there is an element that precedes *Ignorance*, the Buddha did not say. Therefore, we cannot assume that *Ignorance* is the first link in the chain. If we travel the chain in the counter-clockwise direction, we begin with *Old Age & Death* and end with *Ignorance*.

We will start as the Buddha did by asking the question:

"What is the cause of old age and death?"
The answer:
> "There is old age and death because there is *birth*.
> Old age and death are due to *birth*."

Our question to ourselves is:
"What then is *birth*?"

Birth initiates a temporary state of existence in which we suffer the physical and psychological pain of our own making. We live a life of *Dukkha*, due to our *ignorance* of *The Four Noble Truths*.

> How is there laughter, how is there joy,
> with the world burning around you?
> Why do you not seek a light, you in the
> darkness? Look at this dressed-up body,
> covered with wounds, joined together, sickly,
> full of many thoughts. It has no strength, no
> endurance! It is wasted, sick, and frail;
> breaking into pieces, life indeed ends in
> death. In those white bones, …there dwells
> old age and death, pride and deceit.
> - *Dhammapada*: "Old Age" after M. Müller

….

He then asked: "*What is the cause of birth?*"
The answer:
> "There is birth because there is *becoming*.
> Birth is due to *becoming*."

Our question to ourselves is:
"What then is *becoming?*"

Becoming is composed of two elements: the new habits and karmic tendencies that are "created" by us in our current existence, in our current *Ignorance,* plus the karmic compost of previous existences. The new habits and new karmic tendencies are a result of *willful* acts in this existence. *Willful* acts are those acts that are "ego-acts." The "I want it my way" behaviors that we employ to satisfy our *cravings*. These *willful* acts are not in harmony with cosmic law. The karmic compost of previous existences is made up of *willful* acts committed in previous existences that have not been neutralized, made remainder-less. For example, if we use the statement "*What goes around, comes around.*" as a metaphor for neutralized, remainder-less *willful-acts,* then "*What has gone around, has not yet come around.*" would be a metaphor for *willful acts* not yet neutralized, not yet remainder-less.

> "Wanting nothing, with all your heart,
> stop the stream. When the world dissolves,
> everything becomes clear."
> - *Dhammapada*: "The True Master" after T. Byrom

....

He then asked: "*What is the cause of becoming?*"
The answer:
> "There is becoming because there is *clinging*.
> Becoming is due to *clinging*."

Our question to ourselves is:
"What is *clinging?*"

Cling is what honey does to one's finger when one sticks one's finger into a honey-pot. *Cling* is what we do with

58

sense pleasures, views, theories, beliefs, rituals, rules and observances that we "can't live without." Our most insidious *clinging* is to the notion of a "me". This *clinging*, we cultivate for "me" and "mine" is a lot more tenacious than *clinging*-honey and, in the end, definitely not as sweet. We carry a lot of baggage. There is *clinging* resulting from willful acts in this existence and *clinging* resulting from willful acts in past existences. What a mess we have created for ourselves.

> "Those who without clinging to anything,
> rejoice in freedom from attachment, whose
> appetites have been conquered, who are full of
> light, are free in this world and the next."
> - *Dhammapada*: "The Wise Man" after M. Müller
>
> ....

He then asked: "*What is the cause of clinging?*"
The answer:
> "There is clinging because there is *craving*.
> Clinging is due to *craving*."

Our question to ourselves is:
"What is *craving*?"

Craving is defined as compulsion, impulse, impulsion, will, need, obsession, acquisitiveness, avarice, covetousness, cupidity, greed, mania and all of their synonyms.

We all have our *cravings*; at times, hiding in secret places. There is no point in denying this fact. Sit down in a quiet place and ask yourself, for example, the questions: "What can I not live without?" or "What is it, that if someone denied me of it, would cause me to harm them?" Be prepared for mental resistance, anger, lethargy and whatever other defences your mind seeks to deploy to avoid answering, truthfully, questions of the sort you now are asking yourself. *Craving is desire gone bad.* We try to satisfy our *craving* with acts of will – willful acts. It doesn't work. We keep trying because of our *Ignorance – ad infinitum.*

> "He who overcomes craving, difficult to be
> conquered in this world, sufferings fall off
> from him, like water-drops from a lotus leaf."
> - *Dhammapada*: "Thirst" after M. Müller
>
> ....

He then asked: "*What is the cause of craving?*"
The answer:
> "There is craving because there is *sensation*.
> Craving is due to *sensation*."

Our question to ourselves is:
"What is *sensation*?"

Sensation is physical or mental. A stimulus is perceived as a pleasant, unpleasant or neutral *sensation*. A physical *sensation* is the perceived with the physical senses. A mental *sensation* is the perceived with the mind. In Buddhism, the mind is considered to be one of the senses.

We are pleasure-seeking creatures. We desire to perpetuate pleasant *sensations* and to suppress unpleasant *sensations*. This desire to perpetuate or suppress *sensation* leads us into the wasteland of insatiability because desire can never be satisfied – never! Why do we keep trying to satisfy desire, rebirth after rebirth? Isn't there some point in time where we just stop and say: "Wait a minute, I've been repeating this same behaviour, with minor variations, all my life and it always turns out the same. What is going on?"

> "The craving of a thoughtless man grows like a creeper; he runs from life to life, like a monkey seeking fruit in the forest."
> - *Dhammapada*: "Thirst" after M. Müller

....

He then asked: "*What is the cause of sensation?*"
The answer:
> "There is sensation because there is *contact*. Sensation is due to *contact*."

Our question to ourselves is:
"What is *contact*?"

We have six senses: eye, ear, nose, tongue, body, mind. There is a sense object associated with each sense: eye>form, ear>sound, nose>smell, tongue>taste, body>touch, mind>mental-object. The coincidence of eye, form and visual consciousness is called *contact*. This same relationship applies to all the remaining senses. That is, sense + sense object + sense consciousness = *contact*.

Contact and its corresponding *sensation* (feeling) cannot be separated. Once *contact* is established, *sensation* as pleasant, unpleasant or neutral is immediately established. In many cases, their coincidence is life preserving. For example, it keeps one from holding one's hand over an open flame for too long a time. In many other cases, it makes *craving* tough to erase from one's behaviors, past, present and future.

> "He who lives looking for pleasures only, his senses uncontrolled, immoderate in his food, idle and weak, temptation will certainly overthrow him, as the wind throws down a weak tree." - *Dhammapada*: "The Pairs" after M. Müller

He then asked: "*What is the cause of contact?*"
The answer:
> "There is contact because there are *six senses*.
> Contact is due to the *six senses*."

Our question to ourselves is:
"What are the *six senses*?"

The *six senses* are eye, ear, nose, tongue, body, mind. They have their corresponding *sense objects*, exterior to themselves: form, sound, smell, taste, touch, mental object.

The source of our suffering is not due to the *senses* or their corresponding objects. It is our apperception of this raw sense data that is the cause of our pain and misery in this life. One should think twice before literally following the advice: "If thine eye offend thee, pluck it out." It has always been a mind game, but the body seems to take the blame for our ignorant behaviour most of the time. It's the easy way out. After all, it is the mind that is the ring-master in one's personal circus, isn't it?

> "He who is restrained in all things,
> is freed from all pain.
> He who controls his hand, he who controls
> his feet, he who controls his speech,
> he who is well controlled, he who delights
> inwardly, who is collected, who is solitary and
> content, him they call Master."
> - *Dhammapada*: "The Mendicant" after M. Müller

．．．．

He then asked: "*What is the cause of the six senses?*"
The answer:
> "There are six senses because there is *name and form*. The six senses are due to *name and form*."

Our question to ourselves is:
"What are *name and form*?"

Name is defined as the psychological elements of sensation, perception and volitional formations. *Form* is the human body.

> "Understand that the body is merely the foam
> of a wave, the shadow of a shadow."
> - *Dhammapada:* "Flowers" T. Byrom

....

He then asked: "*What is the cause of name and form?*"

The answer:
> "There is name and form because
> there is *consciousness*. Name and form
> are due to *consciousness*."

Our question to ourselves is:
"What is *consciousness*?"

The Buddha said: "Because it cognizes, it is called *consciousness*." Because what cognizes? *Consciousness* cognizes.

Buddhist philosophy spends an immense amount of thought and word trying to make sense out of the Buddha's words: "*Consciousness* isn't our self." We won't do the same. Instead, we will only say, the answer to this question lies in profound *Prajñāpāramitā*.

> "When you become aware of your conditioning you will understand the whole of your consciousness. Consciousness is the total field in which thought functions and relationships

exist. All motives, intentions, desires, pleasures, fear, inspiration, longings, hopes, sorrows, joys are in that field. But we have come to divide the consciousness into the active and the dormant, the upper and lower level — that is, all the daily thoughts, feelings and activities on the surface and below them the so-called subconscious, the things with which we are not familiar, which express themselves occasionally through certain intimations, intuitions and dreams."
- J. Krishnamurti *Freedom from the Known;* Chapter 3

"*When you become aware of your conditioning you will understand the whole of your consciousness.*" That is, when you understand *The Four Noble Truths,* you will understand the whole of your consciousness.

....

He then asked: "*What is the cause of consciousness?*"
The answer:
    "There is consciousness
    because there is *volitional formation.*
    Consciousness is due to *volitional formation.*"

Our question to ourselves is:
"What is *volitional (willful act) formation?*"

As we noted earlier; *willful acts* are those acts that are "ego-acts." The "I want it my way" behaviors, that we employ to satisfy our *cravings*. These *willful acts* are not in harmony with cosmic law.

The Buddha said there are fifty-two *volitional (willful act) formations* (see list below). One can look at this collection of *volitional formations* as the fifty-two drawers of an apothecary cabinet. Each drawer is stuffed, more or less, with a particular *volitional formation*, with a particular *"willful-act" formation*. The entire cabinet stands on a foundation of *Ignorance*. Each *"willful-act" formation* is there as a result of past *good* or *evil volitional acts*. These past *good* and *evil willful acts* are commonly called karma.

The "will" that we exercise in the commission of *good and evil acts* is compounded from *Ignorance* and a measure of *volitional formation* as found in one or more of the fifty-two drawers that constitute the "karma-cabinet." The content of the drawers is ever in flux. We, through our *willful acts*, our *volitional acts*, predicated on *Ignorance*, add and delete karmic content. In other words, we add "cause-and-effect" content — continuously. It is only when an act is *pure*, that is, creating no karma, that the cabinet is not used. It is only when an act takes place without the influence of *Ignorance* or *volition* that it can be called *pure*. It is an act that leaves no traces, much like the track of a bird in flight.

> **Fifty-two volitional formations:** Adaptability of mental properties, Adaptability of mind, Amity, Appreciation, Attention, Balance of mind, Buoyancy of mental properties, Buoyancy of mind, Composure of mental properties, Composure of mind, Conceit, Concentration of mind, Contact, Deciding, Desire to do, Discretion, Disinterestedness, Distraction, Dullness, Effort, Envy, Error, Faith, Feeling, Greed, Hate, Initial application, Mindfulness, Modesty, Perception, Perplexity, Pity, Pleasurable interest, Pliancy of mental properties, Pliancy of mind, Proficiency of mental properties, Proficiency of mind, Psychic life, Reason, Recklessness, Rectitude of mental properties, Rectitude of mind, Right action, Right livelihood, Right speech, Selfishness, Shamelessness, Sloth, Sustained application, Torpor, Volition, Worry. (This is our mental DNA, so to say.)

. . . .

He then asked: "*What is the cause of volitional formation?*"
The answer:
> "There is volitional formation
> because there is *ignorance*.
> Volitional formation is due to *ignorance*."

Our question to ourselves is:
"What is *ignorance*?"
Ignorance is our not understanding *The Four Noble Truths*.
....

The Buddha then studied this chain of cause and effect from the opposite direction and found it to be true.

> *Ignorance*
> is the cause of
> *Volitional Formations*
> is the cause of
> *Consciousness*
> is the cause of
> *Name* and *Form*
> is the cause of
> *Six Sense Faculties*
> is the cause of
> *Contact*
> is the cause of
> *Sensation*
> is the cause of
> *Craving*
> is the cause of
> *Clinging*
> is the cause of
> *Becoming*
> is the cause of
> *Birth*
> is the cause of
> *Old Age* and *Death*.

The chain begins with the element of *Ignorance*. However, the Buddha had never said that *Ignorance* is the causeless cause. He just did not reveal anything before *Ignorance* as a cause. The source of *Ignorance* is hidden from us. We don't understand *Ignorance*. Why should we worry about its source? It should be the least of our worries. We do have a full plate with just these twelve elements, don't we?

The Buddha, once again, speaking on the theme of *Dependent Arising*:

> "Profound, Ananda, is this *Dependent Arising*, and it appears profound. It is through not understanding, not penetrating this law, that the world resembles a tangled skein of thread, a woven nest of birds, a thicket of bamboo and reeds, that man does not escape from the lower realms of existence, from the states of woe and perdition, and suffers from the round of rebirth." - buddhanet.net

Editor's Note: The *Doctrine* is even more "profound" in its English incarnation. As one student of Buddhist philosophy observed: "It would be a good idea to prepare more elegant translations from the Pali and Sanskrit into English." Does English have the capability to express the concepts presented in Pali? Do we have the courage to seek understanding for ourselves?

14

THE FIRST NOBLE TRUTH
Truth of Dukkha

The Buddha was very clear, very scientific in his formulation of the human condition here on earth. Firstly, he stated what the problem is/was: *Truth of Dukkha*. He then followed by stating the cause of the problem: *Origin of Dukkha* and then the solution to the problem: *Cessation of Dukkha* and finally the way to implement the solution: *Path of Liberation from Dukkha*. It can't be any clearer than that. There is no need for outside intervention. The priests and the preachers, the psychologists and the psychiatrists have the same problems as we do. There are no experts available to solve the problem for us. According to the Buddha, it is our job to understand the concepts expressed in *The Four Noble Truths* and in that understanding, transcend our ignorance.

> When we use the word ignorance, we do not mean or mean to imply stupidity. The words are not synonymous.
>
> Ignorant behaviour is the result of being *un*-educated, *un*-aware, or *un*-informed about something or someone. Stupid behaviour is the result of being educated, aware, or informed about something or someone and persisting to behave as if one was *un*-educated, *un*-aware, or *un*-informed about something or someone. Ignorant behaviour is not the result of stupidity. Stupid behaviour is not the result of ignorance.
>
> We use the word *Ignorance* throughout this text to refer to our non-existent understanding of:
>
> Truth of Dukkha
> Origin of Dukkha
> Cessation of Dukkha
> Path of Liberation from Dukkha

Dukkha is the Buddha's definition of the human condition: *Life is Dukkha*. *Dukkha* covers the entire range of the human experience; birth, aging, sickness, death, in all its physical and psychological manifestations. *Dukkha* is more than suffering, anxiety or stress as defined in the Western language lexicons. It is rooted deeper, and it is more pervasive than these words suggest.

We are all swimming in our self-created world of *Dukkha*. We are up to our collective necks in sorrow, pain and confusion. Each and everyone of us has a sad story to tell. Each and everyone one of us was born, and each and everyone of us will die. Why? According to the Buddha, it is because of *Ignorance*. Ignorance of what? Simply this: we do not understand *The Four Noble Truths*. Therefore, we do not understand ourselves.

> Understanding is not an intellectual pursuit. Right understanding is never intellectual. "Intellectual understanding" is a collection of opinions. There is no such thing as "I think I understand." You either do understand, or you don't understand. It is not a brain-game. Right understanding is experiential, and that is the way we use the word in this text.

The Buddha broke the concept of *Dukkha* down into its various facets. Each of these facets must be understood if one is to be free of its effects.

According to the Buddha, *Dukkha* manifests as:
- ordinary suffering,
- a result of change,
- a result of conditioned states (the *Five Skandhas*).

The first aspect of *Dukkha* concerns our physical make-up, our form, our body. The second and the third aspects relate to our mental make-up. In actuality they overlap each other; they do not stand alone. Very often, we find that the

Buddha slices the pie, so to say, in many pieces to make it a bit easier to handle. Making it bite-size so one can chew and digest the ideas presented without suffering mental indigestion.

....

14.1 ORDINARY SUFFERING

This facet of *Dukkha* concerns the eternal cycle of physical suffering. It is associated with birth, growing old, illness and death. Intuitively, we all know this cycle to exist. We see nature going through its four seasons. We plant new seeds in the spring, and we pull out the dead plants in autumn. We walk in the woods and marvel at the spring flowers and the decaying wood all in the same moment. We watch the bees flitting from flower to flower and see them exhausted and dying in late autumn. We see our loved ones grow old and die. We accept it all as the natural cycle of life except when it comes to ourselves. Why? According to the Buddha, the answer is — our ignorance.

> "All the world's a stage,
> And all the men and women merely players;
> They have their exits and their entrances,
> And one man in his time plays many parts,
> His acts being seven ages. ...
> Last scene of all,
> That ends this strange eventful history,
> Is second childishness and mere oblivion,
> Sans teeth, sans eyes, sans taste, sans everything."
> - William Shakespeare "*As You Like It*": Act II Scene VII.

And "sans everything" we leave this world none the wiser for why we were ever born into it. What strange beings we are — sleepwalking, jousting with shadows, fearful of each other. How many lifetimes will it take before we awaken?

The Buddha had remembered all of his past lives on the night of his Enlightenment. He remembered his "sleep-walking, jousting with shadows, fearful of each other" life experiences and he went beyond them. He demonstrated to us that it is doable.

The *Jātaka Tales*, a collection of "birth stories," record hundreds of the Buddha's past lives as a human, a god, or an animal. They make for fascinating reading.

> "Vainly I sought the builder of my house
> Through countless lives. I could not find him...
> How hard it is to tread life after life!
> But now I see you, O builder!
> And never again shall you build my house.
> I have snapped the rafters, Split the ridgepole
> And beaten out desire. And now my mind is free."
> - *Dhammapada:* "Old Age" T. Byrom

....

14.2 CHANGE

Take a minute to mentally catalog the things in your life that have not changed. Can you do it? Even the memories of the things you say have not changed – have changed. They have been modified, rearranged, maximized or minimized depending on who you think yourself to be today.

Nothing in this world stands still, but many of us continue to spend a lot of time, energy and resources trying to keep, forever, the things we enjoy and dismiss the things we do not enjoy. Whether it be an overstuffed closet full of yesterday's plush toys or a mind overstuffed with memories of things that, in actuality, were never really so grand; we are master collectors. I am those things I collect. They define who I am. I do not wish change because it makes me insecure and so my closets get bigger and fuller.

We think of ourselves as the master manipulators of our environment. We go to the moon. We go to the bottom of the oceans. We manipulate genes. We create robots to replace ourselves. We search for the beginning of eternity. We search for civilizations on other planets. We bow to the god of science. We worship the god of money. We serve the god of war and destruction. We kill each other over skin color, belief systems or tribal customs. We do not accept change as the natural flow of Reality. We will have it our collective way. We are doomed to fail, and we fail every time because the world does not dance to our music. Just think about it. History is littered with our catastrophic failures. And still we persist and suffer as a result. Why? According to the Buddha, the answer is – our *ignorance*.

> There is a stream close by and the children of the town love to play there. They wade into the water and build barriers, dams out of stones, sticks, leaves and mud to keep the water from moving downstream. No matter how hard they try to control the stream, the water finds its way through their constructions and soon washes away the entire assemblage.
>
> Once in awhile, some older children stop by to tell the young dam builders that they were a lot more successful in damming the water for longer periods of time. They wax eloquent about the dams they had created in days-gone-by and laugh politely at the efforts of their younger colleagues. When allowed, by the younger dam builders, to show examples of their prowess as dam builders, the older generation does not fare appreciably better than the present lot in their constructions.

"The only thing that is constant is change."
- Heraclitus

If we are at all conscious of what transpires in our daily existence, *Dukkha as ordinary suffering* and *Dukkha as a result of change* are easy to see. The Buddha is telling us that even though we are confronted each moment with this suffering and change, we do not see it for what it is. We do not see that we are the source of our suffering. We do not see it for what it is because of our *ignorance*. We suffer the pain of loss or change, but we cover it up with self-medication of one sort or another. We do not deal with it. We hide from it in a self-induced fog of psychological and physical placebos.

> A friend of mine recently suffered a significant loss. It was a massive, life-changing event. His friends counseled him to seek professional help to get over the psychological trauma of the event, even if it meant taking psycho-pharmaceuticals. Others counseled him just to forget the whole thing and get on with his life. "Find a suitable distraction, a hobby, for example," they told him. And yet others counseled him to give up the loss to God. "Let God fix it," they said. He decided against all of these well-meaning, bound-to-fail approaches.
>
> What did he do? He did nothing. He sat down somewhere quiet whenever the enormity of the loss overwhelmed him and let the pain of it engulf him. He let the sorrow and misery flow over him like a great tsunami wave. He did not run from the pain, and he did not run to the pain. He did not get angry. He did not blame circumstances. He did not blame someone. He did not analyze it. He did not try to rationalize it. He just, literally, sat in the pain of it.
>
> Masochistic? Hardly. He found that by sitting in this psychological pain, the pain soon dissipated. It was empty. It was his self-created hell that he was sitting in, and it had no substance other than the substance he had given it. It had no importance other than the importance he had given it. He sat in the chaos of his loss and survived; knowing he would not know such pain again. He knew this not intellectually but as a deeply grounded "Aha-Erlebnis." He did not have a need to analyze, to judge, to conclude anything. His understanding was the result of his experience. The loss was real. There was no denial of that. It was what he did with the fact of the loss that was important. Real understanding is a result of one's experience, and that is the way a bit of ignorance is washed away.

. . . .

14.3 CONDITIONED STATES – THE FIVE SKANDHAS

The Buddha defined the *Five Skandhas* as Form (Rupā), Sensation (Vedanā), Perception (Samjñā), Volitional Formation (Samskāra) and Consciousness (Vijñāna).

The *Five Skandhas* are the five aspects that comprise our entire physical and mental existence. We exist only in terms of these five elements. The *Skandhas* are conditional. They only exist because of other conditions and those other conditions only exist because of other conditions. That is why the *Skandhas* are called "empty." We are a series of causes and effects. There is no "me" other than what arises at this exact moment due to the interplay of the *Five Skandhas*. This is what the Buddha found. This is what the Bodhisattva Avalokiteshvara proclaimed in the *Heart Sutra*. There is nothing in this world that is not a conditional arising. There is nothing in this world that is permanent. Everything in this life is impermanent, fleeting, "Fata Morgana-ish." It has no root.

We seek permanence in the impermanent, and what we experience is a deeply rooted, hard to fathom, discontent. This deeply seated discontent is called *Dukkha*.

We spend a lot of our energy cultivating roots in quicksand, trying to create and maintain permanence in our lives. We have our traditions, our philosophies, our belief systems, our history, our nationalism, our families, our tribes, our "this" and our "that" but they are all products of thought. The product of our collective thinking. Our collective thought goes back countless ages. It gives us a false sense of continuity, of permanence. Thought is always there to fill the hole of our discontent, our rootlessness, our aloneness, but it never lasts. It can afford us momentary comfort until one sees, out of the corner of one's eye, the fleetingness of it all. How many cohesive, compatible, contradictory, factual, non-sensical, scattered, self-centred thoughts have you had today?

The doctrine of the *Five Skandhas* is not something to be read, and dis/agreed with and then conveniently stuffed into some mental drawer. These words are telling you that, in Reality, you don't exist as Sally or Sam or John or Jane. You are a creation of the mind. Think about this, if you dare. We are process, and process means movement and change. How much of you is the same as it was a week ago, a month ago, a year ago? — both physically and mentally.

> "All that we are is a result of our thought:
> the world is founded on our thought,
> it is made up of our thought."
> - *Dhammapada:* "The Pairs" after M. Müller

The original "Self" — the state of non-ignorance — can only be seen/experienced in *Prajñāpāramitā*. When the mental constructions fall away one *clearly* sees the *Five Skandhas to be empty*. When thought is still and silence reigns one sees *one's original face*.

> "Without thinking good or evil,
> in this very moment,
> what is your Original Face?"
> - Zen Master Enō

The Buddha tells us that we can do this. One can see *one's original face*. One can experience this "falling away" of mental constructions for oneself. When will I stop "thinking good or evil," making judgements, formulating opinions, busying the mind with trivialities? I ask myself again: "Why am I too busy to discover this state for myself? Why am I still making excuses? When will I look into my *Original Face?*"

15

THE SECOND NOBLE TRUTH
Origin of Dukkha

The origin of Dukkha is *craving*:
- for pleasurable sensory satisfactions and an aversion to those which are not pleasurable,
- to be someone or something in this life or the next,
- to not-be someone or something in this life or the next.

One can say that *craving* is *desire* gone mad.

Craving affects body and mind. We are pleasure-seeking manifestations, and desire is part and parcel of our normal existence. *Craving* causes us to adopt behaviors that are totally egocentric. There is nothing about craving that is of any value to anyone. It is an example of "me" at my worst. It separates us from the world, from other beings, from our original self. *Craving* leads to clinging. When we cling to something or someone, we have become totally rudderless. We are puppets on a string. We have abdicated.

Sensory satisfaction is a standard human expectation and, it can be argued, a necessary condition for our existence. Would we eat or drink if whatever we ate or drank had no taste or caused stomach pains or worse? Would we procreate if the act of procreation was without its tender moments? Would we look into a summer sunset if our eyeballs became toasted in the process? Would we bother to smell a rose if its smell made our noses itch and our eyes water? Would we read poetry or study mathematics?

When does desire become craving? Intuitively, we may know the answer to this question. The problem is, with many of us, that we do not want to answer the question to ourselves. Where or what is the tipping point for "me" when eating one piece of chocolate is only an invitation to eat the remaining contents of the box?

Who "wills it" that the second piece of chocolate is soon to be in my mouth? This *willing,* this act of volition is a cognitive process by which we commit to a particular course of action. In this case, it is to devour the chocolate. It is not "accidental." It is purposeful. We put "our" mental-muscle into the accomplishment of the purpose. It means the ego is fully engaged. It means the universe has now been downsized to the diameter of "me." It means, that again, for umpteenth time today, I have dropped out of the world-as-it-is and fallen into the world of as-I-want-it-to-be.

Craving is not limited to the physical senses. Craving also has a mental dimension, because the mind is considered, in Buddhism, to be one of the senses. This mental dimension manifests in our need "to be or not to be" someone or something.

What would it be like if one were a doctor of medicine but one was called "plumber of medicine"? And what if the plumber was called "doctor" instead? Would this affect the quality of medicine? Would this influence the quality of plumbing? The desire to excel in the art of healing people or plumbing is one thing. The desire to excel in what one perceives to be the societal, psychological trappings that accrue to one being called "doctor" or "plumber" is something else altogether, isn't it? To excel in the healing arts whether it be people or plumbing is based on factual knowledge, and it is not tainted by ego. To excel in being called "doctor" or "plumber" is, in part, dependent on what society attributes to the word "doctor" or "plumber."

Examine your reactions to these words. What is your personal relationship to these words? Who does one become when someone addresses one as "doctor" or "professor" or "Your Honor" or whatever? Who does one become when one is introduced to someone with a title before their name? Titles before one's name and an alphabet soup (BS, MS, Ph.D., ad nauseam) appended to one's name is the "stuff" of egos. Egos, to survive, need ever-increasing doses of the "stuff" that keeps them in their prime.

It is here where fact and fancy collide. The desire to be a healer coming into conflict with the desire to emulate the lifestyle of a doctor. We miss the tree for the forest, much like the monk in the following story:

> Two monks were once traveling together. They were walking down a muddy road in heavy rain.
>
> Coming around a bend, they spied a lovely woman. She was unable to cross the mud-filled intersection.
>
> The older of the two monks lifted the woman in his arms and carried her across the muddy intersection and set her down on the walkway again. The monks then went on their way, and the woman went her way.
>
> The younger of the two monks observed the action of the older but said nothing. He did not speak again until that night when they reached their lodgings. Then he no longer could restrain himself. "We monks don't go near females," he told the older man. He went on, "It is dangerous. Why did you do that?"
>
> "I left the woman there, at the intersection," said the older man. " Are you still carrying her?"

How often do we find ourselves in circumstances similar to that of the young monk, where, in his case, *to be a monk* took precedence over *to be in the moment*? The young man took on the trappings of being a monk just as we take on the trappings of doctor, plumber, father, mother, wife, husband. It is what we think we should act like when in a situation, according to what we are called, rather than acting from clarity and anonymity. These *cravings to be or not to be*, these runaway desires, are karmically toxic.

> Karma is a word that has come to mean everything to everybody. There is good karma. There is bad karma. I win the lottery and credit it to my good karma. You win the lottery, and I credit that to my good karma and your bad karma. It is bad for you because all the winnings will cause you to create more bad karma. It is good for me because the opportunity to create bad karma is not there.
>
> Karma is neither good or bad. We make the distinction "thinking" that we know something, but our "knowing" is only a demonstration of our ignorance.
>
> Karma is cause and effect. Karma is: "What goes around, comes around." Karma is: "There is no free lunch." Karma is: "You reap what you sow."
>
> Karma is created as the result of our *willful acts*. A *willful act* is an expression of our "limited" consciousness. It is an act (in thought, word, or deed) done for our benefit. It excludes rather than includes. It excludes because it is an expression of "me" and, by definition, "me" excludes. Therefore, it is an act that is not in tune with cosmic law because cosmic law is not exclusive.
>
> "If a man speaks or acts with an evil thought,
> pain follows him, as the wheel follows the foot of the ox that draws the carriage. ...
> If a man speaks or acts with a pure thought,
> happiness follows him,
> like a shadow that never leaves him.
>
> 'He abused me, he beat me, he defeated me, he robbed me,'
> — in those who harbour such thoughts
> hatred will never cease.
>
> 'He abused me, he beat me, he defeated me, he robbed me,'

> — in those who do not harbour such thoughts
> hatred will cease.
>
> For hatred does not cease by hatred at any time: hatred ceases
> by love, this is an old law."
> - *Dhammapada:* "The Pairs" after M. Müller

Any act of volition, this expression of the "I want it my way" behaviour, this *act of will,* just adds more to the karma compost heap.

We see Reality from a minuscule, fragmented, egocentric perspective. We cause a shambles in the world around us because we want it our way — all the time.

When one is angry, does one know the hectares of psychological geography one poisons with one's anger? When one decides to cheat the public transportation system out of a fare, does one understand the repercussions one has set into motion? When one belittles one of one's many social media friends, does one know the extent of the injuries one produces?

Even if one does not unleash one's venom on one's friends, even if one does pay the bus fare, one has created karma just in the thoughts associated with the, in this case, undone acts. Because one has willed these behaviors in one's thinking them; because one has intended these behaviors; because one has applied one's personal agenda to the "what is" — karma has been created.

These behaviors are rooted in who we think we are. They are rooted in the "me" and "mine." Do we have any idea of how we are going to clean up this mess? Do we think an apology for our anger will do it? Do we think that sending the bus company an anonymous donation will do the job? Do we think that sending our social media friend a box of chocolates may neutralize the karma? We have changed the resonance of the universe with our selfish, intended, willful, behaviour. Do we think gifting a box of chocolates will set it right again?

> You love animals. You donate money regularly to various animal shelters. You are very proud of the fact that you support the work of these shelters. You tell yourself; "It is a good act. I'm doing some-thing worthwhile." There is a sense of pride in you. It is a confirmation that you are a "good" person. The act has a high feel-good quotient attached to it. Unfortunately, it is also a karma producing action. Why?
>
> The vicarious satisfaction you take in hearing you tell yourself: "It is a good act. I'm doing something worthwhile." is the culprit. It's not really about the animals, is it? It's about you. "Look at me," I say to myself: "Look at what a fine person I am." Even if you share this opinion with no one but yourself, you have added another piece of karmic baggage to your collection. We must stay continually aware of our intentions, our agenda. Unfortunately, we are on "automatic pilot" most of the time. Many of us are not aware that these "good acts" stem from selfish motives.
>
> Why don't we just donate the money and forget about it? Is it necessary to polish our "fine person" image? Why do we do this? What are we looking for? What are we *craving*?

16

THE THIRD NOBLE TRUTH
Cessation of Dukkha

"Stop your craving," he smilingly tells me.
"Just give up it up," he advises me.
"Tell that to someone addicted to smoking, drinking, eating, sex, their social network, their belief systems, their Forex trading account, the idea of Enlightenment or the myriad of other useless pursuits enshrined in this society," I tell him.
"Just cut the cord," he persists.
"You're crazy," I tell him, laughing a bit hysterically.

To end *Dukkha*, one must end *craving*.

It is a long road to Buddhahood, and I've just hit the first of many brick walls in the journey. Up until now, it has been all fun and games reading about *Dukkha* and its source and its effects but now I've got to act. And it is now that I begin to find out who I am. And it's now, that all the walls of self that I've created over my lifetime are starting to shake and quake; and the fault lines are beginning to show; and soon I will see that I am nothing but a chimera, a Fata Morgana, and then what will I do?

Don't do anything. Let the walls fall where they may. You will build new walls to replace the ones that fall. That is the way we function. Watch how this works. Stay alert to the shifting sands-of-self. Do not expect anything to happen, but be assured that things will happen. Don't look back. Looking back just refreshes where you thought you were no longer. It just strengthens the past. It's an old mind trick, and we fall for it quite often. We are interested in a *remainder-less* fading and the ending of craving. The key word here is *remainder-less*, without remainder, in other words, karma neutral — devoid of cause and effect. It is only *remainder-less* when you leave it in the dustbin. If you say: "Yes, thankfully, I am rid of it", you are not rid of it!

Is there anything we do that is *remainder-less*? Is there any experience we have had that leaves no trace, no residue, no memory? We automatically catalog everything in our memory banks, don't we? That is the way the brain works. It records raw sensory input. Our minds give this sensory input *meaning* according to our volitional formations. This *meaning* manifests itself as our ideas, opinions, philosophies, beliefs, and preferences concerning everything under the sun. When some of these *meanings* reach a pleasurable critical mass, that is, when they give us more pleasure or more satisfaction than others, they become cravings. *Desire gone bad.*

Broadly speaking, we have a factual memory and an ego-supporting psychological memory. One cannot separate the two. They are intertwined like a bowl of cooked spaghetti. The factual memory contains "things" we need to remember to survive on this planet, for example, $1+1=2$. The psychological memory contains "things" like the memory of the math teacher that taught me sums. He was a tyrant/gentleman and this thought of him still makes me angry/happy. Why do I still have this thought about him?

Our heads are full of these "*remainders*" which serve as reminders as to who we think we are. Each of these *remainders* is a brick in the wall that hinders our "seeing" the Reality that is just beyond the wall. Each of these *remainders* is a part of what I call "me." Why is it important to hang on to a piece of trivia about a math teacher who has probably long since turned into chalk dust? Why does this man still exercise control over me, from beyond the grave? What is important here: the message ($1+1=2$) or the messenger (the math teacher)?

One cannot "will" these *volitional formations* away, because in the "willing" one only strengthens the *volitional formation*. It must fade-away to become *remainder-less*. For something to fade-away it must not be fed and it must not be starved. Just let go of it, leave it and don't go back to see if it is gone. Just move on. Remember that 1+1=2 and drop the attendant drama.

> One sees a beautiful spring flower and what does one do? One looks for its name in one's memory; time passes. The look-up function, one's internal google-system, drags up a name, but one is not sure it is correct; time passes. Now one begins feeling guilty because one can no longer remember the name of a flower; time passes. One is no longer looking at the flower. In fact, one may have started walking away from it. But one's brain is still working on the flower's identity and also on excuses for one's blatant stupidity because one could not remember the flower's name. Why does one consider oneself to be stupid if one cannot remember the name of a flower? What does this "blatant stupidity" do to one's image of one being a "flower-name-knower?"
>
> The residue of this unsuccessful flower-naming game is now in one's brain. It, this residue, will be modified and included into one's self-image. One will either make excuses for one's faulty memory, blaming it on outside circumstances of one sort or another; or one will try to bury the experience in some subconscious dustbin; or one will sign-up to take a junior college course in "*Flower Naming for Flower Name Forgetters.*"
>
> However, one will never ask oneself: "Why do I need to know the name of the flower? Why can't I just look at it?" One will never see this charade for what it is: a *craving* to be something or someone — *to be* an expert *or not to be* a dummy.
>
> Until we begin seeing this flower-naming incident as an example of our ever present thought patterns; as an example of the type of mind-chatter that we are always engaged in; as an example of our mental life, day-in and day-out; we are doomed to *Dukkha*.
>
> Only when we begin to live our lives in awareness of what is going on about us without formulating an opinion, making a judgement, coming to a conclusion, will we go beyond the state of *Dukkha*. No one cares what your opinion is; why do you?

In the overall scheme of things, all of us, experts and dummies, wind up in the same place. Isn't there something more important in this life than these trivial pursuits? This constant grooming of our Fata Morgana egos is a dead-end, both literally and figuratively.

Spend more time being quiet. Spend more time in passive awareness. Spend more time alone, in meditation. Spend more time watching the grand charade that runs through your mind without trying to manage it. Over time, it will begin to fall apart, without remainder.

17

THE FOURTH NOBLE TRUTH
Path of Liberation from Dukkha

It is said, that the Buddha while *actively engaged in Prajñāpāramitā*, "saw" an ancient path. A way that has been trodden many times before by Buddhas past and present. This narrow way had a name; it was called *The Noble Eightfold Path*. It is the *Path of Liberation from Dukkha*. It is composed of the following elements:

Right View,
Right Intention,
Right Speech,
Right Action,
Right Livelihood,
Right Effort,
Right Mindfulness,
Right Meditation.

The eight elements begin with the word *Right*, which is translated as *skillful, wise* or *wholesome*.

Although it is called *The Noble Eightfold Path*, it is only *one path* with eight named components. It can be compared to a "stranded electrical cable" which consists of individual strands of copper wire bound within an insulated casing. The bundle of strands is considered to be one electrical path. All the elements of the *Eightfold Path*, its strands, exist in parallel to one another, in contact with one another, in support of one another, dependent on one another and not hierarchal to one another.

Although it is called the *Eightfold Path*, it is *not a path*. It does not have a beginning, and it does not have an end. One doesn't begin "here" and one doesn't end "there." Each of the "strands" is a guide and not a goal. All of the strands are in play simultaneously but not necessarily all to the same degree. Our ignorance, our lack of understanding offers a resistance. Some of the strands are more accessible than others in the early stages of engagement. One can see this for oneself when one engages the *Eightfold Path* in one's life.

For example, *Right View* has to do with the wisdom to see things the way they are. And to see things the way they are presupposes an understanding of *The Four Noble Truths*. To truly understand *The Four Noble Truths*, one must experience *The Four Noble Truths* for oneself; this is a matter of insight. To cultivate the state known as insight, one must involve *Right Effort*, *Right Mindfulness* and *Right Meditation*. It is these three "*Rights*" that prepare the mind for deep insight into the nature of "what is." *Right View* is also supported by *Right Speech* and *Right Livelihood*. *Right Speech* and *Right Livelihood*, for example, caution against killing by word, thought or deed thereby helping to mitigate suffering. As *Right View* unfolds it supports the other seven elements.

The elements of the *Path* come together like the notes of a symphony come together. They dance together like fireflies on a warm summer night. They reflect and refract each other as the jewels in Indra's net. They are, together, as complete as the experience of a falling snowflake on a cold winter day. *The Noble Eightfold Path* is the expression of ancient law. It is "what is — as it is" and not "what is — as I would have it be."

"Truth is a Pathless Land." - J. Krishnamurti

The Buddha said that in following this *Path of Liberation* he came to direct knowledge of what we now call *the Doctrine of Dependent Co-arising* The Buddha calls on us to follow this *Path of Liberation*. Why do we hesitate? Why do we procrastinate?

There is a story called the *Parable of the Poisoned Arrow*. It addresses the problem we mortals have about staying with the matter at hand and, unlike the Buddha, meandering off into speculative territory asking questions that need not be asked. The story goes something like this.

There was a monk called Malunkyaputta. He seemed dissatisfied with what the Buddha was teaching. One day, when he was exceptionally "full of himself" he challenged the Buddha by stating that unless he, the Buddha, revealed the answers to some unanswered questions (which the monk enumerated) he, Malunkyaputta, would leave the Sangha and find himself another teacher. Malunkyaputta had thrown down the gauntlet, and the Buddha responded in a way that dismantled Malunkyaputta in short order. The Buddha not only reminded the monk that he had never said he would answer questions of this nature, but he also said that answers to questions such as these were of no value when it came to gaining an understanding of The *Four Noble Truths*. The Buddha then went on to tell the story of a man who had been wounded in battle by a poisoned arrow:

> The wounded warrior's friends rushed him to a doctor to attend the wound. The warrior, however, would not allow himself to be treated until he knew everything there was to know about the man who had shot him. Was the archer a nobleman, a priest, a heretic? What was the archer's name, his tribe, his family name? Was he young or old? He then wanted

to know all about the arrow that had caused the wound, its construction, the wood it was made of, the nature of the poison and on and on. His friends pleaded with him to stop with the questions and allow the doctors to tend to his wound. He would not hear of it. He went on asking futile questions. And then he died, having learned nothing.

It is said Malunkyaputta got the message and did not leave the Sangha.

Moral of the story? Get your priorities straight. Deal with the problem at hand. Stop the speculations. The problem is *Dukkha*. Deal with it.

Are you curious about the nature of the questions that Malunkyaputta wanted to be answered? Well, here is a list of a few of them:
1. Is the world eternal? …or is it not?

2. Is the world finite? …or is it not?

3. Is the self identical with the body? …or is it not?

4. Does the Buddha exist after death?…or does he not?

(Do you have any questions you would like to add to the list?)

Using *The Noble Eightfold Path* as a metaphor for "Roadmap of Life" is one way to approach the eight elements it contains. If we overlay our life journey with these eight elements, we can get a pretty good idea of the way our lives should be conducted to get from the mythical-here to the mythical-there. By being skillful in the application of the elements contained in the *Eightfold Path* we can, theoretically, break the chain of *Dependent Co-arising* at its most accessible point — *Craving*!

> "Our pleasures are extravagant and luxurious;
> sunk in lust and looking for more,
> we undergo birth and death.
>
> Men and women,
> driven on by craving,
> run about like trapped rabbits;
> held in fetters and bonds,
> they experience pain for a long time, again and again.
>
> Wise people do not call that a strong fetter which is made of iron, wood, or hemp; far stronger is the pleasure found in possessions.
>
> That fetter wise people call strong which drags down, will yield, but is difficult to undo; after having cut this, at last, one leaves the world, free from cares,
> leaving cravings behind."
> - *Dhammapada:* "Thirst" after M. Müller

18

PUTTING IT ALL TOGETHER
the Heart Sutra verse by verse

Now it is time to bring together the various and diverse threads that have been presented in the previous seventeen chapters. Very early on, we diverged from our stated goal of discussing the *Heart Sutra*. Instead, we launched into discussions about some of the Buddhist concepts that are expressed in and are the foundation of the *Heart Sutra*.

We also spent time adding new words to our vocabulary with, hopefully, sufficient explanations of their meaning in the context in which we were using them. We redefined familiar words in the context of what we were discussing (e.g. empty and Emptiness) because the original *Heart Sutra* was not written in the English language.

> What is the language of the earliest extant copy of the *Heart Sutra*? It is written in the Chinese language on palm-leaf. The manuscript itself was found at the Horyuji Temple, and dated to 609 CE.

The scholars that translated the Chinese logograms, where each symbol expresses a concept, were constrained by the limits imposed by the "translated into" language (e.g. English). Translation from one language to another language is not merely a *one for one* word substitution.

It is well-known that many of the ideas expressed in the Sanskrit language have no western language (e.g. English, German) counterparts. The Indian "mind" developed expressions for matters more of a spiritual nature, whereas, the Western "mind" developed expressions for concepts mainly of a material nature.

Words are not exact. Words do not have only one meaning. Words carry a patina that is based on time, culture, belief, politics and a host of other factors.

Even if the original language of the *Heart Sutra* were written in English, we would need to look closely at the meaning of words that were written over fourteen hundred years ago. For example, the first three lines of the well-known Lord's Prayer as written in old English:
>Fæder ure
>ðu ðe eart on heofenum
>si ðin nama getalgod

To suitably present the various concepts that underpin the *Heart Sutra* we have spent words discussing the *Doctrine of Dependent Arising, The Four Noble Truths* and *The Noble Eightfold Path*. We did that using our newly acquired vocabulary.

Because these Buddhist ideas did not just arise out of thin air, we then had to discuss from whence they did arise. That journey brought us a bit of biographical background on Shakyamuni Buddha, Avalokiteshvara, Shariputra, and some of the minor, yet necessary, actors in this story of the *Heart Sutra*.

In the case of the Buddha and Avalokiteshvara, we tried to give the reader a "word picture" of the deep states of meditation from which their profound insights issued.

> You are sitting comfortably. Your body is in balance. Your spine is straight. You are not leaning forward, backward or to the side. Your breath is natural in rhythm and volume. You breathe exclusively through your nose. Your joined hands rest comfortably in your lap. Your eyes are not entirely open, and they are not entirely closed. Your gaze is "loosely" focused on the floor before you. Your face is soft. You are not frowning or

tensing your facial or neck muscles. You bring your mental focus, without changing your physical state, to the inhale and exhale of the breath. You mentally observe your breath without trying to change it. Your mental observation is based on the sound of the breath and the physical sensation of bodily movement. You do not concentrate on watching the breath. You just watch it as a casual observer. Your eyes, you casually observe, have lost their focus. The floor is no longer a floor. Unless, of course, you "will it" to be a floor again. But you are just casually observing, so you don't care what it is, do you? (Interesting isn't it? It becomes a floor only when I call it by name.) The sound of your breath is slowly receding. You do not panic. You continue observing. You find that the tactile sense that determines your body dimensions, that is the amount of "space" you occupy, is dropping away. There "seems" to be a "feeling of openness." This feeling of openness extends over the entire body. You get the sense that you are expanding, not because you are getting larger but because you are becoming finer, more gossamer as if borders were disappearing. You are just observing. You still sense your breath as a bodily movement, but even that sensation is becoming less and less. You stay with the breath and then somewhere along the line, even the sense of it drops away. The observer is gone. Thinker and thought are gone. Where are you now? That is not a possible question, is it? It presupposes a *you*. Is there a *you*, when the observer is gone?

You blink your eyes, and you recognize the blinking. You hear your breath, and you recognize your breathing. You look at the clock and find unaccountable time has passed since the moment you first sat down. Where did the time go? You had no sense of time passing, not that you were interested, in any case. Do you have any words that you would like to pass on to others regarding "your time away?"

We talked about the fact that any words that Avalokiteshvara used to express the state of *Prajñāpāramitā*, the state of Perfected Transcendent Wisdom, he had experienced, were inadequate. He had to use words to convey his insights to people that had no experience of *Prajñāpāramitā*. He used the best words he had; the Buddha's words as expressed in the *Doctrine of Dependent Arising, The Four Noble Truths* and *The Noble Eightfold Path*.

Let us now look at the *Heart Sutra* with a mind that has acquired a bit of a background in the concepts unique to Buddhist thought.

"The Bodhisattva Avalokiteshvara actively engaged in Prajñāpāramitā, ..."

The word *Prajñāpāramitā* is difficult to define in western languages. In Sanskrit: *Prajñā* = wisdom and *pāramitā* = perfected. The Bodhisattva was actively engaged in a state of *Perfected Wisdom*. *"Actively engaged"* means he was not in a mindless trance. He was awake and alert, but he was beyond the world of thought.

....

"... clearly saw the Five Skandhas to be empty, thus completely overcoming Ignorance."

In this state of perfected wisdom, *"clearly saw"* can be considered the equivalent of *to have understood*. He understood the *Five Skandhas* as conditional. He understood that skandhas exist only because of conditions; that means, they are empty; they are rootless; they are impermanent. *Ignorance* is the result of our non-understanding of the *Five Skandhas*. If we understand *Five Skandhas* as conditional, *Ignorance* is overcome.

In our present state of *Ignorance*, of non-perfected wisdom, the skandhas exist "as real". For us, they have the quality of being not-empty.

> "Eaten alive
> by lice and fleas
> — now the horse beside my pillow pees."
> Haiku-Master Matsuo Basho

"O Shariputra, form is no other than Emptiness. Emptiness is no other than form. Form is exactly Emptiness. Emptiness is exactly form."

The Bodhisattva now tells Shariputra that form is no other than the Absolute Reality; it is no other than *Emptiness*. If form were other than the Absolute Reality, other than *Emptiness*, it would mean that the Absolute Reality was not absolute. Then he adds *Emptiness (is) no other than form*. Which is exactly the way we, in our state of *Ignorance* "see" Absolute Reality (*Emptiness*). We see the Absolute Reality (*Emptiness*) as form. *Form* and *Emptiness* are exactly the same; it all depends on one's perspective. From the perspective of *perfected wisdom*, one sees form as *Emptiness*. From the perspective of *non-perfected wisdom (Ignorance)*, one sees *Emptiness* as form. They fit each other exactly. Look around, do you see anything in your view that is not form?

....

"The same is true for sensation, perception, volitional formations, consciousness ..."

"*The same is true*" means: s*ensation* is no other than *Emptiness*, *Emptiness* no other than *sensation*; *perception* is no other than *Emptiness*, *Emptiness* no other than *perception*; *volitional formations* are no other than *Emptiness*, *Emptiness* no other than *volitional formations*; *consciousness* is no other than *Emptiness*, *Emptiness* no other than *consciousness*.

> "My horse
> Clip-clopping over the fields — Oh ho!
> I too am part of the picture!"
> Haiku-Master Matsuo Basho

"O Shariputra, all dharmas are forms of Emptiness; not born, not destroyed, not stained, not pure, without loss, without gain."

In Buddhism, *Dharma* is defined as "cosmic law and order". Whereas "*dharma*" (small "*d*") is defined as a thing, a phenomenon. That is, *dharmas* are objects of the senses.

Avalokiteshvara told Shariputra that *all dharmas* are *forms* of *Emptiness*. The only place *forms* of *Emptiness* are "real" is in our state of *non-perfected wisdom* where we "see" *Emptiness* as *objects of the senses*.

Avalokiteshvara had already told Shariputra that "*... form is no other than Emptiness. Emptiness is no other than form. ...*" and that the same *"is true for sensation, perception, volitional formations, consciousness ... ."* Sensation, perception, volitional formations, consciousness are *forms of Emptiness*. He now repeats these statements when he tells Shariputra that "*all dharmas are forms* (things, phenomena) *of Emptiness.*"

It is only in our state of *non-perfected wisdom*, only in our dualistic state, that "*dharmas*" are born/destroyed, stained/pure, with loss/gain. We cannot "see" *Emptiness* as anything other than a *thing*, a *phenomenon*, a *form*. Our everyday view of reality is from the view of opposites. *Emptiness* does not have an opposite. It is not dualistic. If it were dualistic, it would be conditional. If it were conditional it would be both the subject and object of "cause and effect." Emptiness embraces cause and effect, contains cause and effect but it is not subject to cause and effect. It is "not two" and it is "not one." It just is.

When Avalokiteshvara makes the statement "*not born, not destroyed, not stained, not pure, without loss, without gain*" he effectively places the word "*dharmas*" into its proper perspective by stating they are *not born* and *not destroyed*. If a *dharma* is *not born* and *not destroyed* is it a thing? Is it a phenomenon? What is it? Is it not just a name? A name for something we take for being "real" because of our state of *non-perfected wisdom*?

> "Zen maintains a stance of "not one" and "not two," i.e., "position-less position," where "not two" signals a negation of the stance that divides the whole into two parts, i.e., dualism, while "not one" designates a negation of this stance when the Zen practitioner dwells in the whole as one, while suspending judgment in meditation, i.e., non-dualism. Free, bilateral movement between "not one" and "not two" characterizes Zen's achievement of a personhood with a third perspective that cannot, however, be confined to either dualism or non-dualism (i.e., neither "not one" nor "not two"). " - Stanford Encyclopedia of Philosophy; *Japanese Zen Buddhist Philosophy*

. . . .

"In Emptiness, there is no form, no sensation, perception, volitional formations, consciousness; no eye, ear, nose, tongue, body, mind; no color, sound, smell, taste, touch, phenomena; no realm of sight, no realm of consciousness;"

Everything we think we are is bogus. Why? Simply because we think we are that which we-think-we-are. We exist in ignorance of our true being.

> "This is how to contemplate our *conditioned* existence in
> this fleeting world: like a tiny drop of dew,
> or a bubble floating in a stream;
> like a flash of lightning in a summer cloud,
> or a flickering lamp, an illusion, a phantom, or a dream.
> So is all *conditioned* existence to be seen."
> *The Diamond Sutra*

"... no ignorance and no end to ignorance; no old age and death, and no end to old age and death; no suffering, no cause of suffering, no extinguishing, no path; ..."

In *Emptiness*, the state of perfected wisdom, there is *no ignorance*.

If there is *no ignorance*; there can be *no end to ignorance*.

If there is *no old age and death*; there can be *no end to old age and death*.

If there is *no suffering* (*The First Noble Truth*); there can be *no cause of suffering* (*The Second Noble Truth*).

If there is *no suffering*; there can be *no extinguishing* of suffering (*The Third Noble Truth*).

If there is *no suffering*; there can be *no path* (*The Fourth Noble Truth*) to the *extinguishment* of *suffering*.

....

"... no wisdom and no attainment."

There is *no wisdom*. There is no knowledge and no acting on knowledge. *Prajñāpāramitā* is beyond wisdom. There is no *attainment* because there is nothing to be attained. The desire for *attainment* is *craving* by another name.

>"The journey itself is my home."
>Haiku-Master Matsuo Basho

....

"No attainment and thus the Bodhisattva lives Prajñāpāramitā, with no hindrance in the mind, no hin-

drance, therefore, no fear, far beyond deluded thoughts, this is Nirvana."

Can we do this "none-doing"? Can we *live Prajñāpāramitā*?

....

"All past, present, and future Buddhas live Prajñā-pāramitā, and, therefore, realize unexcelled complete Enlightenment."

Are you ready to put your name on the list of *future Buddhas*?

....

"Therefore know, Prajñāpāramitā is the great mantra, the vivid mantra, the best mantra, the unsurpassable mantra; it ends all pain."

There does not seem to be a single definition for the word *mantra*. It is a two syllable Sanskrit word where the first syllable is *man* = "to think" and the second is *tra* = "tool or instrument." It can be defined as an "instrument of thought". It can be anything, a phrase, a sound, a syllable, or a word. It doesn't necessarily have to have any meaning. It is used in every religion, in every spiritual practice and also in a lot of very successful commercial advertising campaigns.

It is an instrument of thought and therein lies its worth and its worthlessness. In most cases, the worth of a *mantra* is inversely proportional to its frequency of recitation. The more one recites a *mantra*, the more the *mantra* becomes ritualized. The worthlessness of a *mantra* is directly proportional to its ritualization. A *mantra* should be a seen as a steppingstone or as "a finger pointing at the moon." It is a temporary means and not an end. It should be used as a guide and not as a goal.

> A colleague of mine who was spiritually inclined had a guru. The guru told him that whenever things were going well or things were not going well he should recite a mantra. The mantra he told him to recite is very well known and highly respected for its authority and power. The mantra goes like this: "*Om Mani Padme Hum.*"
>
> My colleague was caught up in the recitation of this mantra. Many times while we were working on a team project together, I would see his lips moving silently reciting the mantra. When things were difficult, he would recite the mantra audibly. The bigger the problem, the louder the recitation of "*Om Mani Padme Hum*" would become.
>
> One day, while listening to his mantra litany as a response to a problem the development team was busy with, I asked him if he thought that his mantra mumbling was going to solve the problem at hand. No response. I asked him if the recitation was reducing his agitation and his frustration, as it was most certainly, increasing mine. No response. I then asked him if the recitation was helping him think more clearly about various problem-solving strategies. No response. The last question I asked him was whether or not he thought that this mantra chanting was supposed to create a magic spell that would banish the problem at hand. The last question I had asked was the proverbial "straw that broke the camel's back." He stood up from the work table and announced, somewhat distraught: "You certainly do not seem to appreciate what I was trying to accomplish." Then he left the office for the day. The rest of the team eventually solved the problem, and the world was, again, in order.
>
> The next morning, the mantra-man, as he had come to be known, was at his desk when I arrived. We nodded our greetings and without any other words the work day began. From time to time, I would glance his way, as casually as possible, hoping to get a reading on how he felt after yesterday's fiasco. The only thing I noticed was that his lips were not moving in their usual, rote, recitation fashion.

The clock soon was pointing to "lunchtime." We spoke our first words then. He asked whether I'd be interested in a bit of lunch, maybe a sandwich. It was there, sitting on the lakeshore, throwing crumbs to the swans floating by, that I casually mentioned not seeing his lips moving in silent recitation this morning. To my relief, he began to smile. He pulled out a piece of paper from his shirt pocket and handed it to me. I unfolded the paper and there in bold block print was written:

> "It is very good to recite the mantra Om Mani Padme Hum, but while you are doing it, you should be thinking on its meaning, for the meaning of the six syllables is great and vast."
> - 14th Dalai Lama

Having read it, I handed it back to him. And he, still smiling said: "I had forgotten the part where it says: *'You should be thinking on its meaning, for the meaning of the six syllables is great and vast.'*"

We were out of crumbs to feed the floating swans. They had floated on to someone else.

....

"This is the truth, not a lie."

This statement applies only to the author of the statement. We, do not know this to be true and accepting it as true is meaningless. We must realize "*truth*" for ourselves.

....

"So set forth the Prajñāpāramitā Mantra, set forth this mantra and say: ... "

Yes, *set forth this mantra* but do not forget what the Dalai Lama has said:
> "You should be thinking on its meaning,
> for the meaning... is great and vast."

"Gate! Gate! Paragate! Parasamgate! Bodhi Svaha! Prajñā Heart Sutra."

"Gate! Gate! Paragate!"
    Gone, gone, gone beyond!

"Parasamgate!"
    Gone beyond the "gone beyond!"

"Bodhi"
    Perfected Wisdom,
    beyond all possible experience and knowledge.
    Awakening!

"Svaha!"
    So be it!

"Prajñā Heart Sutra."
    The great path for the perfection of wisdom.

> Gone, gone, gone beyond!
> Gone beyond the "gone beyond"!
> Perfected Wisdom, beyond all possible experience and knowledge. Awakening! So be it!
> The great path for the perfection of wisdom.
> ....

But it is not in the words. It is never in the words. It is in the doing. It is in action and not in re-action. As Seng-ts'an, the Third Chinese Patriarch, said so eloquently:

> "Words! Words! The Way is beyond language,
> for in it there is no yesterday, no tomorrow, no today."
> *Hsin-hsin Ming: Verses on the Faith-Mind*
> Translated by Richard B. Clarke

19

WHAT'S NEXT?

Sit down in a quiet corner and review what you have just been reading. Focus on the Buddha. A human being. An extraordinary human being. One of the few exceptional beings the world has seen. Think about the Bodhisattvas; as persons committed to following the way of the Buddha.

Now review the words of the Buddha and the Bodhisattva. Try and imagine how difficult it is to put the wordless into words. Try to imagine the Buddha spending forty-five years of his life bringing wordlessness into words. Try to imagine the thousands of people that heard these words. Try to imagine how many of them just walked away, either to look for something that "suited them" better or who were too busy getting on with their life of misery to be bothered. Try to imagine the few that found their direction, their compass, in the words and deeds of the Buddha. Try to imagine how these people, over the ages, have been slowly and steadily moving in the direction, if there is such a thing as "direction" toward Bodhisattvahood, Buddhahood. Could it be that you are one of them? Could it be that you have "awoken" in this life as, maybe, you had awakened at the time of the Buddha, or in other previous ages? Who is to say? It may be all speculation; and maybe it is not.

There is a core within us all that resonates with the words contained in *The Heart Sutra, The Four Noble Truths, The Eightfold Noble Path, The Doctrine of Dependent Arising.* This resonance goes contrary to what much of society promulgates as having worth, as having value. It was not any different when these words were announced by the first Buddha. It was not any different when these words were stated by Shakyamuni Buddha, and it won't be any different when the next Buddha makes his/her appearance. This world is *what it is*, and we try to make it into *what it is not* because we think we know better. We are not here by accident, and we are not here to change the world. We are here to change ourselves. It is as simple as that.

In Buddhist Cosmology, a human rebirth is said to be extremely rare. It is said to be as rare as the likelihood of a blind turtle rising from the bottom of an ocean once every one hundred years and putting his head through the hole in a Lifesaving Ring floating on the surface of the ocean. It is also generally said that if one doesn't make a mess out of one's present life, the chances of human re-birth are better the next time around. Sort of like the hole in the ring increasing in diameter or maybe the turtle gaining a bit of eyesight. Of course, no one really knows except maybe the turtle, and it hasn't said a word.

One thing is sure, you have invested time, energy, and thought into this book. That in itself should tell you something. Listen to your heart. Listen to your clear mind.

> "Be A Light Unto Yourself."
> - J. Krishnamurti

May your life go well.

20

HEART SUTRA
complete
(but broken done into bite-size chunks)

The Bodhisattva Avalokiteshvara actively engaged in Prajñāpāramitā, clearly saw the Five Skandhas to be empty, thus completely overcoming Ignorance.

O Shariputra, form is no other than Emptiness. Emptiness is no other than form.

Form is exactly Emptiness. Emptiness is exactly form. The same is true for sensation, perception, volitional formations, consciousness.

O Shariputra, all dharmas are forms of Emptiness; not born, not destroyed, not stained, not pure, without loss, without gain.

In Emptiness, there is no form, no sensation, perception, volitional formations, consciousness; no eye, ear, nose, tongue, body, mind; no color, sound, smell, taste, touch, phenomena; no realm of sight, no realm of consciousness; no ignorance and no end to ignorance; no old age and death, and no end to old age and death; no suffering, no cause of suffering, no extinguishing, no path; no wisdom and no attainment.

No attainment and thus the Bodhisattva lives Prajñāpāramitā, with no hindrance in the mind, no hindrance, therefore, no fear, far beyond deluded thoughts, this is Nirvana.

All past, present, and future Buddhas live Prajñā-pāramitā, and, therefore, realize unexcelled complete Enlightenment.

Therefore know, Prajñāpāramitā is the great mantra, the vivid mantra, the best mantra, the unsurpassable mantra; it ends all pain. This is the truth, not a lie. So set forth the Prajñāpāramitā Mantra, set forth this mantra and say:

Gate! Gate! Paragate! Parasamgate! Bodhi Svaha! Prajñā Heart Sutra.

21

Maka Hannya Haramita Shingyo
(The Heart Sutra)
(Recitation version based on the Chinese logograms.)

KAN JI ZAI BO SA GYO JIN HAN NYA HA RA MI TA JI
SHO KEN GO ON KAI KU DO IS SAI KU YAKU.

SHA RI SHI SHIKI FU I KU KU FU I SHIKI.

SHIKI SOKU ZE KU KU SOKU ZE SHIKI JU SO GYO SHIKI
YAKU BU NYO ZE.

SHA RI SHI ZE SHO HO KU SO FU SHO FU METSU FU KU
FU JO FU ZO FU GEN.

ZE KO KU CHU MU SHIKI MU JU SO GYO SHIKI MU GEN
NI BI ZE SHIN NI MU SHIKI SHO KO MI SOKU HO MU GEN
KAI NAI SHI MU I SHIKI KAI MU MU MYO YAKU MU MU
MYO JIN NAI SHI MU RO SHI YAKU MU RO SHI JIN MU KU
SHU METSU DO MU CHI YAKU MU TOKU I MU SHO TOK
KO.

BO DAI SAT TA E HAN NYA HA RA MI TA KO SHIN MU
KE GE MU KE GE KO MU U KU FU ON RI IS SAI TEN DO
MU SO KU GYO NE HAN.

SAN ZE SHO BUTSU E HAN NYA HARA MIT TA KO TOKU A
NOKU TA RA SAM MYAKU SAM BO DAI KO CHI HAN NYA HA
RA MI TA ZE DAI JIN SHU ZE DAI MYO SHU ZE MU JO SHU
ZE MU TO TO SHU NO JO IS SAI KU SHIN JITSU FU KO.

KO SETSU HAN NYA HA RA MI TA SHU SOKU SETSU
SHU WATSU:

GYA TEI GYA TEI HA RA GYA TEI HA RA SO GYA TEI
BO DHI SOWA KA .

HAN NYA SHIN GYO

Glossary

*of common and uncommon
words found in this book*

Aha-Erlebnis: "Aha-experience" which gives a sudden insight. Coined by German psychologist Karl Bühler.

Arahant/Arahatā: "one who is worthy" or is a "perfected person."

Ascetic: a person who dedicates his or her life to a pursuit of contemplative ideals and practices. Siddhārtha practiced a very extreme version of asceticism for six years before he gave it up for the "middle way."

Asana: a hatha yoga posture.

Avalokiteshvara: in Buddhism, and primarily in Mahayana Buddhism, the Bodhisattva ("buddha-to-be") of infinite compassion and mercy, one of the most popular of all figures in Buddhist Cosmology. Also known as Chenrezig, Guanyin, Kannon, Kanzeon Bōsatsu, Kuan-yin, Kuze Kannon, Lokeshvara et al.

Basho, Matsuo (1644-1694)**:** the most famous poet of the Edo period in Japan. Today, he is recognized as the greatest master of haiku.

> A caterpillar,
> this deep in fall –
> still not a butterfly.
> - Matsuo Basho

Benares: now known as Varanasi, is a North Indian city on the banks of the Ganges in Uttar Pradesh. It is one of the oldest continuously inhabited cities in the world. As the spiritual capital of India, it is the holiest of the seven sacred cities of Hinduism and Jainism. Many have said that it is only a gossamer-like curtain that separates the material world from the spiritual world in Varanasi.

Bodh Gaya: a religious site and place of pilgrimage near the Mahabodhi Temple in Gaya. It is where the Buddha achieved enlightenment under the bodhi tree.

Bodhi: is also called enlightenment, realization, awakening, insight into transcendental truth.

> "You are all Buddhas
> There is nothing you need to achieve.
> Just open your eyes."
> - the Buddha

Bodhisattva (bodhi = enlightenment + sattva = being)**:** In early Buddhism, the term was used to refer specifically to the Buddha in his former life. Today it refers to someone who is motivated by great compassion.

Boom-box: a disgustingly loud stereo, usually battery-powered and small enough to be carried on one's shoulder while walking. The little brother of a Ghetto Blaster.

Brahmin: Hindu caste; specializing as priests, teachers and protectors of sacred learning across generations. They were responsible for religious rituals in temples, as intermediaries between temple deities and devotees, as well as rites such as solemnizing a wedding with hymns and prayers.

Buddha: one who is awake to reality.

Buddhist Cosmology: the description of the universe according to Buddhist scriptures and its associated commentary. The view of the world presented in Buddhist cosmological descriptions is not consistent (nor was it meant to be) with astronomical data. It is the universe as seen in the state of perfected wisdom (*Prajñāpāramitā*).

Byrom, Thomas: translated the *Dhammapada* in a particularly poetic fashion. Shambala Publications has published his work in the *Shambala Pocket Classics* version. Highly recommended.

CERN: the European Organization for Nuclear Research,

Channa: Prince Siddhārtha's servant and charioteer. He explained to Siddhārtha the sight of an elderly man, a sick person, a funeral and an ascetic. He later became a disciple of the Buddha and eventually an arahant.

Clarke, Richard B. (1933 - 2013): American Zen teacher. Translated the Hsin Hsin Ming into English. The translation is, by far, one of the most poetic and accessible versions of the text authored by the 3rd Chinese Patriarch.

Consciousness: "When you become aware of your conditioning you will understand the whole of your consciousness. Consciousness is the total field in which thought functions and relationships exist. All motives, intentions, desires, pleasures, fear, inspiration, longings, hopes, sorrows, joys are in that field. But we have come to divide the consciousness into the active and the dormant, the upper and lower level – that is, all the daily thoughts, feelings and activities on the surface and below them the so-called subconscious, the things with which we are not familiar, which express themselves occasionally through certain intimations, intuitions and dreams.

We are occupied with one little corner of consciousness which is most of our life; the rest, which we call the subconscious, with all its motives, its fears, its racial and inherited qualities, we do not even know how to get into... It seems to me that it is as trivial and stupid as the conscious mind — as narrow, bigoted, conditioned, anxious and tawdry." - J. Krishnamurti *Freedom from the Known;* Chapter 3

Dalai Lama: a monk of the "Yellow Hat" school of Tibetan Buddhism. He is considered to be the successor in a line of teachers who are believed to be incarnations of Avalokiteshvara Bodhisattva. The name is a combination of the Mongolic word "dalai"="ocean" and the Tibetan word བླ་མ་ (bla-ma)="guru, teacher, mentor."

Desire: "One of the factors in consciousness is *desire*. From perception, contact and sensation, thought creates the image and the pursuit of that image is the *desire* to fulfill, with all the frustration and the bitterness following from that. Now, can there be an observation of sensation not ending in *desire*? Just to observe. Which means one has to understand the nature of thought, because it is thought that gives continuity to *desire*; it is thought that creates the image out of sensation followed by the pursuit of that image." - J. Krishnamurti *The Wholeness of Life;* Pt. II; Ch. 15

Dhammapada: a collection of the sayings of the Buddha in the form of verse. It covers a variety of themes and is an excellent way to approach the Buddha's teachings. The verses are crystal-like in their construction and meaning. There are many versions of the *Dhammapada* in print and on the internet.

Dharma: has many meanings in Indian philosophy. It all depends on whether one is reading a Hindu, Buddhist,

Sikh or Jainist text. And as with many Sanskrit words, there is no simple translation for the word into western languages. In all incarnations of the word, it relates to "the right way of living" or "cosmic law" or "righteous path." It can also mean the teachings of someone like the Buddha. It is a *huge* word in that it includes everything in this universe and beyond. Nothing stands outside of this word. In Buddhism it is defined as "cosmic law and order" and it also refers to the teachings of the Buddha.

Diamond Sutra: a dialogue between the Buddha and Subhuti that seeks to answer the questions posed by Subhuti. The Sutra ends with this beautiful verse;
"So I say to you -
This is how to contemplate our conditioned existence in this fleeting world:
Like a tiny drop of dew,
or a bubble floating in a stream;
Like a flash of lightning in a summer cloud,
Or a flickering lamp, an illusion, a phantom, or a dream.
So is all conditioned existence to be seen.
Thus spoke Buddha."

Doctrine of Dependent Arising: "When there is this, that comes to be; with the arising of this, that arises. When there is not this, that does not come to be; with the cessation of this, that ceases."

Dukkha: the Buddha's definition of the human condition; Life is *Dukkha*. *Dukkha* covers the entire range of the human experience in all of its physical and psychological manifestations. *Dukkha* is more than suffering or anxiety or stress as defined in the Western language lexicons. It is rooted deeper, and it is more pervasive than these words suggest. *Dukkha* is deeply rooted discontent. Neither thought, prayer or any other mental construction will uproot this discontent.

Empty: often used in a sentence as; the quality of being empty. Example: Form has the quality of being empty. It means: form is conditional. It is impermanent. It does not mean that form does not exist. It means that we do not properly understand how it exists because of *Ignorance*.

Emptiness: defined as the Ultimate Reality. It is the underlying principle. It is this universe and every other universe discovered and undiscovered and beyond. It is everything. There is nothing outside of Emptiness. It is inconceivable, and CERN is not going to conceive it. Unless that is, they discover the state of *Prajñāpāramitā*. Emptiness is "full of stuff" that is considered to be something — like form, or like consciousness, or like the "big bang", or like Higg's boson, but it is none of these. It just is — period.

Enlightenment: see "**Bodhi**."

Fata Morgana: a mirage.

Ganges: "… The Ganges, above all, is the river of India, which has held India's heart captive and drawn uncounted millions to her banks since the dawn of history. The story of the Ganges, from her source to the sea, from old times to new, is the story of India's civilization and culture, of the rise and fall of empires, of great and proud cities, of adventures of man … " - *Discovery of India;* Jawaharlal Nehru

Guru: a religious teacher and spiritual guide in Hinduism (original definition). Currently defined as "teacher or guide that you trust."

Heraclitus (ca. 540 - ca. 480 bce)**:** Greek philosopher.
"No man ever steps in the same river twice."
"Much learning does not teach understanding."
"The sun is new each day." all quotes from - brainyquote.com

Huineng (638-713)**:** a Buddhist monk who is one of the most prominent figures in Chan (jap.:Zen) Buddhism. He has been traditionally viewed as the Sixth and Last Patriarch of Chan Buddhism. The *Platform Sutra* of the Sixth Patriarch is attributed to him. It cites and explains a broad range of Buddhist scriptures; *Diamond Sutra, Lankāvatāra Sutra, Mahāparinirvāna Sutra, Mahāprajñā-pāramitā Sutra, Brahmajāla Sutra, Vimalakirti Sutra, Lotus Sutra*, and others.

Indra's Net: has a multifaceted jewel at each vertex. Each jewel is reflected in all of the other jewels. It is used to describe the interconnectedness of the universe.

Ignorance: is the state of our normal, everyday existence. It is the state of non-*perfected wisdom*. It is due to our non-understanding of *The Four Noble Truths*.

Inkin: is a hand-held bell used to mark periods of zazen (sitting-meditation).

Jātaka Tales: stories of the previous births of the Buddha, in both human and animal form. He appears in them as a king, an outcast, a god, an elephant etc. In each form, he exhibits some virtue that the tale illustrates.

Kalama, Alara: a hermit saint and a teacher of yogic meditation. After Siddhārtha had become an ascetic, he went to live with Alara and his disciples. Among other things, Alara taught him a mantra and visualization meditation method called "dhyānic" meditation.

Kapila: a Vedic sage credited as one of the founders of the Samkhya school of Hindu philosophy.

Kapilavastu: the city where Siddhārtha Gautama was raised and lived until he left the royal compound and began his life as an ascetic. The exact location of Kapilavastu is not known. Some say that it is located in Southern Nepal, west of Lumbini. Others say that Kapilavastu is situated in Northern India. The city was sanctified in the memory of Kapila, who had lived some 200 years before the Buddha. It is said that the Buddha was well versed in the philosophical tenets taught by Kapila.

Kapok: fibers from the ceiba tree that are used as a filling for meditation sitting cushions and life-preserver vests among other things.

Karma: a Sanskrit term that means "action" or "doing." In the Buddhist tradition, karma refers to action driven by intention (will) which leads to future consequences. Those intentions are considered to be the determining factor in the kind of rebirth in Samsāra (see: **Samsāra**), the cycle of rebirth.

> It is said the Buddha was once asked: "What is the cause, what is the reason, O Lord, that we find amongst mankind the short-lived and long-lived, the healthy and the diseased, the ugly and beautiful, those lacking influence and the powerful, the poor and the rich, the low-born and the high-born, and the ignorant and the wise?" The Buddha's reply was: "All living beings have actions (*karma*) as their own, their inheritance, their congenital cause, their kinsman, their refuge. It is *karma* that differentiates beings into low and high states." - buddhanet.net

Krishnamurti, Jiddu (11.05.1895-17.02.1986)**:** It was twenty odd years ago when I first "found" Krishnamurti, by chance, in a used-book store; under the title *The First and Last Freedom*. He has been "reading his books" to me ever since. I say *reading* because he has a way of speaking directly to one. He can create a space where two minds communicate without hindrance. His writing reminds me of the Buddha's sutras; impeccable logic; precise words; probing, at times disquieting, questions. J.K. stresses that we must take the journey of self-enlightenment for and by ourselves. We are responsible for who we are and where we are bound. It is an uncompromising stance; spoken by someone that has "seen" *what is, as it is*. He once said; "*Truth is a Pathless Land*". Having said it, he spent the rest of his life trying to show us the magnificence of the journey.

> There are many websites that feature J.K.'s works in pdf format, or audio tape. If one is interested in J.K.'s works, I would recommend "The First and Last Freedom" as a good place to begin.

Lotus posture: a cross-legged sitting asana in which the feet are placed on the opposing thighs. It is used for meditation, in numerous traditions. It is said to resemble a lotus. It encourages proper breathing and offers physical stability.

> The full lotus asana is difficult for many people. Do not entertain the idea that one cannot meditate unless one can sit in full lotus position. It is a mind trick to think so; do not fall for it.

Lumbini: The birthplace of Siddhārtha Gautama.

Müller M. (1823-1900)**:** Friedrich Max Müller; a German-born philologist and Orientalist; lived and studied in Britain for most of his life. He wrote on the subject of Indology. The *Sacred Books of the East* was prepared under his direction. (Ed. Note: This is a treasure of unbelievable worth. It is in the public domain.)

Magadha: an ancient kingdom of India, situated in what is now west-central Bihar State, in northeastern India. It was the nucleus of several larger kingdoms or empires between the sixth-century BCE and the eight-century CE.

Maha: great. For example, *Mahabodhi* = great awakening.

Meditation: "Meditation is one of the most extraordinary things, and if you do not know what it is you are like the blind man in a world of bright colour, shadows and moving light. It is not an intellectual affair, but when the heart enters into the mind, the mind has quite a different quality: it is really, then, limitless, not only in its capacity to think, to act efficiently, but also in its sense of living in a vast space where you are part of everything. Meditation is the movement of love. It isn't the love of the one or of the many. It is like water that anyone can drink out of any jar, whether golden or earthenware: it is inexhaustible. And a peculiar thing takes place which no drug or self-hypnosis can bring about: it is as though the mind enters into itself, beginning at the surface and penetrating ever more deeply, until depth and height have lost their meaning and every form of measurement ceases. In this state there is complete peace not contentment which has come about through gratification but a peace that has order, beauty and intensity. It can all be destroyed, as you can destroy a flower, and yet because of its very vulnerability it is indestructible. This meditation cannot be learned from another. You must begin without knowing anything about it, and move from innocence to innocence."
- J. Krishnamurti *Meditations;* 1969; Part 4

Mudra: a symbolic hand gesture used in meditation.

Nairañjanā River: the river (present-day Lilaja River) that flows northward towards the Ganges, passing near Bodh

Gaya. Siddhārtha practiced austerities for six years on the shore of this river in the forest near the village of Uruvela.

Nirvana: extinguishing of *Dukkha*, extinguishing of *ignorance*. *Dukkha* exists because we do not understand *The Four Noble Truths*.

Paragate: gone beyond.

Pāramitā: perfection.

Parasamgate: gone beyond *Paragate*.

Photoshop: an image editing computer program.

Prajñā: wisdom.

Prajñāpāramitā: is defined as "*Perfected Wisdom*." A state that transcends all knowledge and experience.

Samsāra: means literally "continuous movement." It is the endless cycle of birth and death that arises from our not understanding *The Four Noble Truths*.

Sangha: the family of Buddhist practitioners.

Seeing/Saw: used in this book as *insightful awareness*.

Shakya (ca. 600bce): a small independent state located at the foot of the Himalayas. Kapilavastu (see: **Kapilavastu**) was its capital city. The Shakyas were a warrior clan (Kshatriya caste). (Shakyamuni Buddha: the Buddha from the Shakya tribe.)

Shariputra: one of two chief male disciples of the Buddha. The Buddha declared him to be a true spiritual son.

Skandha: an aggregate or a "heap." There are five "heaps" that comprise our entire physical and mental existence. We exist only in terms of these five aggregates. The Buddha defined the *Five Skandhas* as Form (Rupā), Sensation (Vedanā), Perception (Samjñā), Volitional Formation (Samskāra) and Consciousness (Vijñāna).

Sutra: is a type of religious literature present in many Asian traditions. Originally they were oral traditions. In Buddhism, *sutra* refers explicitly to the Buddha's teachings.

Svaha: "so be it".

Thought: "What do we mean by idea? Surely idea is the process of thought, is it not? Idea is a process of mentation, of thinking; and thinking is always a reaction either of the conscious or of the unconscious. Thinking is a process of verbalization which is the result of memory, thinking is a process of time." - J. Krishnamurti, *Collected Works*, Vol. VI, p. 260

Understanding: is experiential. It is not mentation.

Volitional formation: ch-13, *Doctrine of Dependent Arising*

Yashodharā: wife of Siddhārtha Gautama was born on the same day in the same month as Siddhārtha. She was wedded to her cousin when both were in their sixteenth year. At the age of 29, she gave birth to their only child; a boy named Rāhula; an Arahatā; died at age seventy-eight, two years before Buddha's parinirvana (nirvana-after-death).

Printed in Great Britain
by Amazon